W0232738

PENGUIN BOOKS
The Ivy League Playbook
ATHENA

Athena Education was founded ten years ago by two Princeton graduates to transform the education landscape in India and across the globe. Its mission is to empower high-school students, guiding them to gain admission into elite universities worldwide and build the scholars of today into the leaders of tomorrow. With an exceptional team of consulting and writing experts, in-house research, tech, and art mentors, and a Harvard admissions consultant, it offers personalized one-on-one mentorship. From authentic extracurricular profile development to masterful college applications, Athena is a one-stop source for all things college admissions.

ABOUT ATHENA

Athena Education has established a remarkable track record of success and global reach in the realm of college admissions:

- **Global Impact:** Athena has served students from 21 diverse countries, reflecting its international prestige and effectiveness.

- **Proven Results:** Over the past decade, Athena has celebrated more than 3,400 acceptances, with over 900 in 2024 alone.

- **Unmatched Success in 2024:** This year, virtually every Athena student secured admission into their university of choice, including esteemed institutions like Princeton, Stanford, Columbia, Brown, Oxford, and Cambridge.

- **Distinguished Alumni:** Since 2014, over 750 students have successfully navigated the admissions process under Athena's guidance.

- **Elite University Placements:** Athena boasts over 120 acceptances into elite universities, including the Ivy League, Oxbridge, MIT, Stanford, and Caltech.

- **Exceptional Odds:** An international student working with Athena is five times more likely to gain admission to top U.S. universities compared to the average acceptance rates, which can be as low as 1% for international applicants.

This exemplary record underscores Athena's unparalleled expertise in propelling students toward the highest echelons of academic achievement.

ABOUT THE AUTHORS

Rahul Subramaniam, Co-founder
Princeton, 2011

Rahul's academic journey began in Fremont, California, where he not only excelled academically but also thrived as a passionate musician and competitive chess player. His achievements earned him admission to every Ivy-League college he applied to, and he ultimately chose Princeton over Harvard. At Princeton, he pursued a degree in Politics and earned a certificate in Political Economy. Since co-founding Athena Education with Poshak, Rahul has dedicated himself to guiding students through the complexities of college admissions, while helping them discover their unique talents, passions, and life paths. His commitment enables students to realize their highest academic and professional aspirations.

Poshak Agrawal, Co-founder
Princeton, 2012

Poshak excelled at DPS R.K. Puram, graduating in the top 1% of his class and serving as President of the Mathematics Society. As a junior, he was the only student from India awarded a full scholarship to the prestigious Stanford SUMaC summer program. Later, he also received full scholarships to both Stanford and Princeton. At Princeton, he co-led the Entrepreneurship Club while taking rigorous courses in both economics and history. Poshak's professional journey spans from mechanical engineering to finance, equipping him with a broad understanding of global trends. He adeptly uses these insights to guide students on preparing effectively for future challenges and opportunities.

Jared Griffin, Creative Director
Princeton, 2013

Jared Griffin, a literature graduate from Princeton, has served as the Creative Director of Athena's Writing Center since 2018. Specializing in mentoring over 300 students through the overseas admissions process, particularly in crafting their college application essays, Jared brings a distinctive literary flair to each student's work. His passion for creative writing and literature significantly enhances the Athena experience, transforming the journey for budding scholars.

ADVANCE PRAISE FROM PARENTS

Madhusudhan Reddy
Executive Director, Goldman Sachs

"Working with Athena was an absolute game-changer. From the essay ideation to the meticulous final touches, Athena's guidance and expertise were invaluable. Their insightful feedback not only refined the essays but also instilled confidence in our child's abilities. With Athena's help, navigating the daunting college application process became a seamless journey. We are immensely grateful for Team Athena's dedication and passion in helping our kid achieve his academic aspirations."

Sandeep Lodha
Managing Director, Conde Nast India

"Working with the team at Athena was an absolute delight. They managed to establish a great equation with Aanya, one of trust and friendship, while ensuring that task management and decision making on the various line items leading up to the actual application submission was a collaborative process. What was commendable was their commitment to excellence, even if it meant being available with their guidance and support at the 11th hour. Thank you, Team Athena."

Mohd. Haque
Chief Commercial Officer, Americas, Cognizant

"Stellar. If we had one word for Athena's quality of service and results, it would be stellar. From our first meeting, Athena's team was extremely welcoming and eager to bring to fruition all our dreams and wishes. The college application process is a daunting feat, and as a parent who studied in a different education system, we always looked to Athena for guidance. In the essay writing process, Athena was with us every step of the way, from brainstorming ideas, to outlining drafts, to finalizing essays, leaving no stone unturned. However, the help didn't end there. When it came to publishing research, defining the activity list, and choosing the perfect major at each college, Athena never deterred. We are so grateful that Athena was with us in helping our son take the best steps in this process."

THE IVY LEAGUE PLAYBOOK

A STEP-BY-STEP GUIDE TO WRITING WINNING APPLICATION ESSAYS

WRITTEN BY ATHENA

PENGUIN BOOKS

An imprint of Penguin Random House

PENGUIN BOOKS

Penguin Books is an imprint of the Penguin Random House group of
companies whose addresses can be found at
global.penguinrandomhouse.com

Published by Penguin Random House India Pvt. Ltd
4th Floor, Capital Tower 1, MG Road,
Gurugram 122 002, Haryana, India.

Penguin
Random House
India

First published in Penguin Books by Penguin Random House India 2024

10 9 8 7 6 5

ISBN 9780143464389

Typeset in Adobe Garamond Pro by Digiultrabooks Pvt. Ltd
Printed at Thomson Press India Ltd, New Delhi

www.penguin.co.in

Table of Contents

HOW TO USE THIS BOOK

THIS BOOK IS DESIGNED TO MAKE the Common Application Essay process for American undergraduate admissions as simple and effective as possible. In a nutshell, we want to give you the best chance of getting in. And we've written every word with the Indian teenage reader in mind (although their parents can certainly learn a lot, too). Don't treat it as a novel, but as a practical tool: underline, highlight, scribble notes in the margins. Engage with the material. Read it all at once or in chunks. You can even jump around as you wish, but we recommend that you eventually go through everything; you never know from where a creative idea will emerge!

So, *don't skip this overview*. Of course, most people gloss over introductions, but this one's useful. Similarly, don't miss the "Workbook" at the end. It's not some tacked-on appendix to be ignored, rather an invaluable resource and enjoyable way to explore your uniquely individual voice!

Speaking of sections, we have:

- **Overview:** Essential context on the purpose and structure of this book, as well as of the college admissions process. We also mention how you can derive maximum value from your reading experience.
- **Sample Essays:** 25 personal essays that were successful at Ivy League and "Ivy+" universities (e.g. Stanford, Caltech, UChicago), all from Athena's vault of applications over the past few years. Each features the applicant's essay, a detailed commentary to help you understand why their essays were successful, and a writing activity designed to help you start thinking about your own essay. Dive in and do them! Remember: emulate, don't imitate.

- **Workbook:** A simple, comprehensive, step-by-step guide to completing your own personal essay. Each of the three stages—Ideation, Drafting, and Finalization—contains our time-honored tips and tricks for getting the job done well. Our aim is to provide both knowledge and skill, but the only way to build skill is to put knowledge into practice!
- **Glossary:** This book features many industry terms, which we explain here for your reference.

WHAT YOU NEED TO KNOW

Why We Wrote This Book

ELITE AMERICAN ADMISSIONS SYSTEMS SEEM SHROUDED in mystery. Plummeting acceptance rates suggest that even the most stellar academic record no longer suffices to differentiate a candidate from the rest of the applicant pool. The personal essay is an exercise in self-marketing, in underscoring your authentic value-add to a college campus. Without the right frameworks and insights on how to approach this task, many applicants miss the opportunity to convey something profound about themselves. After a decade of studying what works for the world's most selective admissions committees, we've crystalized the elements that distinguish winning essays from those cast upon the dreaded "rejected" pile.

The existing content on this subject, we found, didn't cater to the needs of international applicants, failing to consider their distinct contexts. Thus, these 25 essays seemed like a balanced selection—not too many, not too few. We wish to give readers a fair chance of cracking and developing their own techniques for acing the college essay and unraveling new opportunities in their lives.

Why Application Essays Exist

IF YOU'RE READING THIS BOOK, YOU'VE probably heard lore of this dreaded personal essay, the one piece of writing that must convey all the best parts of you. How you're emotionally resilient, but also vulnerable. Intellectually brilliant, but also curious. How you've surmounted gigantic obstacles, but are still humble. That's a lot of pressure for 650 words, right? Generating an essay topic that encompasses the vast complexity of who you are can be daunting. To write your best essay, you must first understand why it exists and how it relates to the rest of your application.

If the rest of your application is a human body, your personal essay is its heart. It enlivens your grades, letters of recommendation, and activities with the human context they deserve. What are the most formative experiences of your life and how have your perspectives evolved through them? What's your *brand*? What were you put in this universe to do? Answering these questions and conveying them through this genre requires deep introspection and self-awareness.

Admissions officers utilize the personal essay for various purposes. Firstly, they seek to understand the quality and depth of your thought process, especially when faced with diverse, sometimes adverse, circumstances. They're also using this piece to identify your "cultural fit" at their specific university. By evaluating the values displayed in the piece, they'll grasp whether you align with the institution's existing value system and meet the requirements of their incoming freshman class.

Note: admissions officers aren't looking for well-rounded applicants; they seek well-rounded batches, wherein each individual contributes something unique to the community. This essay must exude your specific and unique voice, one that no other similarly-qualified applicant offers. And finally, college admissions officers use essays to glean your grasp of the English language. Thus, each piece you submit must be meticulously proofread and free of any mechanical errors, for this reflects your attention to detail. As the old adage goes, how you do anything is how you do everything.

Also, the American "Common Application Essay" differs from a British "Personal Statement." American universities care less about what you want to study, unless it comprises an essential pillar of your identity. So please don't provide an extended resume of your activities related to computer science or economics. Don't believe us? Here's the latest set of Common Application Essay prompts, so you can see for yourself:

1. Some students have a background, identity, interest, or talent that is so meaningful they believe their application would be incomplete without it. If this sounds like you, then please share your story.

2. The lessons we take from obstacles we encounter can be fundamental to later success. Recount a time when you faced a challenge, setback, or failure. How did it affect you, and what did you learn from the experience?

3. Reflect on a time when you questioned or challenged a belief or idea. What prompted your thinking? What was the outcome?

4. Reflect on something that someone has done for you that has made you happy or thankful in a surprising way. How has this gratitude affected or motivated you?

5. Discuss an accomplishment, event, or realization that sparked a period of personal growth and a new understanding of yourself or others.

6. Describe a topic, idea, or concept you find so engaging that it makes you lose all track of time. Why does it captivate you? What or who do you turn to when you want to learn more?

7. Share an essay on any topic of your choice. It can be one you've already written, one that responds to a different prompt, or one of your own design.

Whether you're the all-rounder or have one pointy passion, there's something above for everyone. But how do you decide which topic or narrative to feature? Well, one strategy is "anti-stereotyping": what skills and sensibilities do you possess that most others from your demographic lack? An Indian girl doing Bharatnatyam—okay. An Indian boy doing Bharatnatyam—tell me more! A boy powerlifting—okay bro. A girl powerlifting—fourth-wave feminism!

The structure of the personal essay can vary greatly based on the content of your story. In fact, your choice of format can display as much personality as your choice of topic. Most often, a narrative structure that follows the arc of Joseph Campbell's *Hero's Journey* is conducive to the type of compelling piece that strikes a chord with admissions committees. This includes you as the protagonist (or "hero") who confronts a challenge or conflict and embarks on a journey of personal transformation to arrive at a higher plane. However, if your story isn't the conventional "growth journey," you may consider alternative structures—anything from a poem or a three-act play to a research brief or even a business plan. Feel free to branch out of the traditional five-paragraph academic paper you're taught to write in school. Have fun with it, but never allow such playful, high-concept formats to obscure the clarity of your message, the key takeaway you'd like to share with admissions officers. Your essay is read quickly in conjunction with the rest of your application, and you cannot risk confusing your reader with too ambiguous of a structure.

Composing this piece of writing is an iterative process, so your first draft can be raw, rough, and rambling. Don't judge yourself! Nonetheless, while writing, here are the specific elements you must convey through your essay. In each of the pieces contained in this book, we discuss the following at length:

1. **Values:** What do you hold dear? What do you never compromise on? What's your internal operating system?

2. **Perspective:** How do you think deeply and differently? What unique points of view do you hold, which may enrich the campus community you eventually join?

3. **Authenticity:** Are you opening your mind and heart? Are you being unapologetically yourself? Do you display fearlessness when it comes to sharing your thoughts and feelings?

4. **Craft:** How clearly, powerfully, *artfully* can you present yourself in writing? Are your sentences free from all grammatical and stylistic errors, and do they spark *delight* in the reader?

Once your story and structure are in place, do also consider the style with which you write, the distinctive literary voice that will help admissions committees get to know the real you. We often recommend that students assume a more American tenor for the comfort of American readers. This includes using American spelling and grammatical conventions. However, this does NOT mean that you rid your essay of cultural artifacts, names, and languages. Instead, you can weave them in while maintaining a style familiar to your reader.

Why You Should Adopt Our Approach

ADMISSIONS OFFICERS SPEND HOURS AND DAYS FLIPPING THROUGH THOUSANDS of essays and have become keenly attuned to sensing authenticity (or lack thereof) in essays. Our approach integrates the creativity and fun of a fictional story with our strategic insights into admissions systems. This essay is neither a professional resume nor a personal diary. The best submissions fall somewhere in-between.

With the advent of generative AI, colleges have become even more sensitive to the authentic voices of students. As we mentioned, your essays are read in conjunction with the remainder of your application; the admissions officers we've spoken with are confident that they can distinguish between scholars who've put in the reflection and work, and those who've taken more convenient paths. Academic integrity is of paramount importance to these institutions.

Note: most students' names have been changed to pseudonyms upon request.

Essays & Summaries

Beatboxing Biophysics: Unraveling Vocal Mysteries

ISH KAUL

Delhi-NCR

Princeton University

"I very much need an anesthetic, Sir."

I found myself seated in the office of Dr. K.K. Handa, one of the top Ear, Nose, and Throat (ENT) specialists in Delhi. Dr. Handa proceeded to spray the contents of a bottle into my nose and mouth. Sour. Burning. Numb. He inserted the stroboscope through my nose, through layers of slime, to its final destination: the supra-glottal region of my larynx. Then, breaking a minute-long silence, he said, "Now, start beatboxing."

This strange journey to Dr. Handa's office began a few years ago. Tom Thum's TEDx video on "vocal percussion" became extremely popular in school. Anyone who could imitate him was revered and granted special status. As a moderately bright teenager, I reasoned as follows: "If cool kids like beatboxing, I would learn to beatbox, and therefore be cool." Guided by this flawless reasoning, I watched every tutorial I could find on YouTube. I also participated in informal beatbox battles with my classmates. I was awestruck that the human mouth was capable of producing such a diversity of sounds, sometimes

3

four of them simultaneously! But as cool as I was becoming, I could not deny my nerdy side: I pondered the physics (biophysics?) of these mesmerizing sounds.

The water drop was created by imitating a Helmholtz resonator with one's mouth and generating pressure waves. The Starsky bass? By vibrating the uvula in the falsetto range. The inward bass...inward base...wait, how was the inward bass produced?

I looked everywhere for explanations of the inward bass. YouTube? No. Books? No. Yes, I even researched on Google Scholar. Nothing. Nothing concrete about the mysterious inward bass, only conjectures from non-specialists. I was incredulous. How did no one in the world know this?

I had to know. This question consumed me. Family, friends, and other well-wishers advised me to let it go, that as long as I could produce the inward bass, that was all that mattered. But I could not let it go! It was my *Moby Dick*, and I its Captain Ahab. After all, how often does there come an opportunity to know something that no one else in the universe knows? (I must admit, that gave me a real kick.) Thus, when all secondary sources proved futile, I decided to conduct some primary research.

Thus began my collaboration with Dr. Handa. He was the only doctor in the entire state with the power to grant me this holy knowledge; only two doctors in Delhi had stroboscopes, and the other worked in a restricted army hospital. So, after asking (OK, begging) his secretary for an appointment, stating that it was a matter of scientific progress, I finally scheduled an appointment for a stroboscopy exam, which entailed inserting a camera attached to the device through my nose to observe my larynx. It was at this moment I started beatboxing, and Dr. Handa, amused, told me how each sound, including the inward bass, was produced. Hurray! I had finally cracked the mystery!

This feeling of possessing exclusive knowledge was not unlike gaining a new superpower. But even more exciting was sharing this new knowledge with the world. This took the form of a website I created with tutorials for around 30 beatboxing sounds and physical explanations, as well as a nice little video of my larynx, courtesy Dr. Handa. I never thought that a casual activity to increase my coolness would spark such an intellectually rewarding journey. In whatever context, from beatboxing to plasma physics to economic philosophy,

I discovered that my deepest impulse is to seek knowledge for its own sake and to give back to society by any means necessary. This hunger for knowledge is my greatest driver, and I cannot wait to continue this journey into deep untrodden forests of new domains in college and life, all the while marching to the beat of my own…mouth.

Summary

ISH WAS AN UNCOMMONLY BRIGHT, ENTHUSIASTIC, and inquisitive physics student with an undeniable academic flair. The problem? So were many kids in his demographic. For American admissions audiences, Indian males are expected to be into STEM. Hence, he needed an angle, what we in the admissions industry call a "hook." What distinguished Ish's profile? Well, it wasn't what you might expect. The two things about him that caught our eye were his intellectual character and quirky beatboxing interest. Combine them, and we could have an essay that caught Admission Officers' eyes as well. The key was that it couldn't be quirky for the sake of being quirky. There had to be *substance*, not just style. Weird + meaningful = interesting + impressive. He'd actually developed a notable project (novel research, under an accomplished physician) around the interest, so it made perfect sense to highlight it.

Values

ONE MIGHT EXPECT A SERIOUS PHYSICS student to take the safe route and remain strictly formal in their story (particularly for Princeton, known to be a fairly stuffy place). Unfortunately, that'd be the wrong move! To separate himself from the crowd of similar Indian male STEMies, Ish needed to showcase his genuine Intellectual Vitality, which is fancy-speak for "love of learning for its own sake." We of course learn to pass tests and get internships, but universities (especially the Ivies!) are bastions of wisdom, seeking to expand human consciousness as a good in itself. They're places for NERDS. Nerds driven by an insatiable "hunger for knowledge." And what's even better is when they simultaneously see their immense curiosity as a means of "[giving] back to society." Just like Ish.

We're sure everyone reading this has at some point met a beatboxer. However, have you met a beatboxer who has emailed dozens of ear-nose-throat (ENT) doctors around Delhi for a chance to peek into their own throat? I doubt it. That's dedication. Hence, we used this narrative to demonstrate Ish's appreciation for the liberal arts*—i.e. the natural sciences, social sciences, and arts, as well as their interdisciplinary intersections—along with his uncommon self-motivation (note how he clearly reads books far outside his primary field of interest). Remember, this scholar is an aspiring physicist. But you rarely see the word "physics" in the essay. Instead, we take one of his offbeat side hustles, then give it some classic Athena spice and sparkle to evoke something far grander than the reader might've expected.

Now, when an Ivy sees that a young man is attempting to *produce* knowledge, not just consume it, their response is, "Wow, this kid would make a really innovative and prolific researcher one fine day. His contributions are going to advance scientific discovery." Ish is a consummate intellectual.

Perspective

AS WE ALWAYS SAY, A GOOD STORY ain't gonna cut it. Similarly, just talking about one's values ain't gonna cut it either. We had to show how Ish's mind worked. The reader needed to see that he was actually capable of some real "intellectual originality," admissions lingo for cleverness and reflection. One of the best ways to leave this impression is to make unexpected connections, such as the link between beatboxing and physics. If you manage to get the reader thinking about something they've never considered before, you've done something right.

Throughout, we see Ish introspecting, self-critiquing, and exercising the scientific method. The ultimate product is something NO ONE IN THE WORLD knows. He used his creative, intellectual capacities to "[crack] the mystery!"; a fundamentally personal discovery that extends beyond the realm of beatboxing to plasma physics and economic philosophy. Harnessing medical equipment to analyze the anatomy of his own vocal cords and understanding the mechanics of each sound also taught Ish to become a better beatboxer and a better scientist. The final paragraph ties it all together.

Authenticity

FROM THE FIRST LINES, IT'S CLEAR that this author isn't afraid to be real. He doesn't take himself too seriously. That's the complete opposite of what AOs expect from the otherwise Standard Strong* Indian male STEM applicant. At no point is Ish detached, opaque, or standoffish. Instead, he's completely transparent, allowing the reader into his thought process and personal failings. The primary tool he uses to achieve this effect is humor, an underutilized—and always welcome—means to convey humanity in application essays. For example, take his simple, unfiltered rationale behind choosing beatboxing in the first place:

1. I want to make friends.
2. To make friends, I need to be cool.
3. Cool people beatbox.
4. I shall beatbox!

Ish doesn't shy away from simply admitting that he's a teenager trying to fit in, like everyone else. That willingness makes him relatable and believable, unlike the many narratives of "perfect" applicants that clutter AOs' inboxes. Most specifically, Ish writes with a distinct conversational tone that appeals to the American reader. It's fun, unpretentious, and energetic—but always undergirded by smart diction and phrasing that reflects a serious applicant. The result? We actually want to meet this guy. (Which is the whole goal of marketing oneself!)

Craft

YOU'LL NOTICE THAT ISH'S ESSAY DOESN'T attempt to be a literary masterpiece with grand poetic flourishes. It's written in a straightforward, direct manner that's always crystal clear. This is a good thing. Many bright young thinkers wish to infuse so many ideas into their essays that the final product ends up overstuffed. Worse, they're so lost in their own heads that their thoughts appear muddled or dense. See how Ish's first paragraph begins with a BANG. He's in the doctor's office (establishing a dramatic setting), doing something weird (which is interesting!). And at the end of the paragraph, we drop a little bomb with beatboxing. The reader can't help but go on! That's what you must achieve with your essay.

Note also the many references and Easter eggs sprinkled throughout. Ish's use of brand names, literary allusions (see the clever throwaway line on *Moby Dick*), and academic jargon captures a feeling of zany, madcap excitement. Such meticulousness functions to keep the story specific. Details are what make or break an essay. He exercises restraint, offering just enough to be impressive without going overboard. Hence, Ish delivers a heartfelt blockbuster instead of an arthouse film: in short, a perfect application essay.

EXERCISE

What are some mysteries that captivate you? If you could unlock a mystery or identify the heretofore unknown answer to a question, what would it be? With the resources at your disposal, how could you go about arriving at that answer?

Wordplay Wizardry: Conquering Language with Scrabble

MEHUL ARORA

Delhi-NCR

Stanford University

"HI! PERHAPS I CAN TAKE YOU to your mother? Where is she?"

"She is outstanding," I awkwardly replied.

The flight attendant giggled.

In all honesty, eight-year-old me was gutted and could not bear the embarrassment of ridicule. I spent the remainder of the flight berating myself for my incompetence with words.

Memorizing dictionary entries taught me nothing about their practical usage. I was unaware of the context and application appropriate for each word, and hence could not employ them. My journey up the proverbial mountain was replete with chasms, and sometimes progress appeared impossible. I was constantly flummoxed by the ease with which my classmates switched between languages and was terrified of becoming a laughingstock if I asked for help in something so basic.

While my struggle persisted, my classmates worshiped the wordsmith of the class, Shaurya. And so did I. He was everything I wanted to be: clever, knowledgeable, smooth—the Word Wizard.

However hard I tried, I could never match his esoteric vocabulary and flowery turns of phrase.

One fine day, a teacher approached Shaurya to be a part of a Scrabble competition in school. Even as I rooted for him along with the rest of my classmates, I toyed with the idea of competing myself. I was already the word Muggle; I had nothing to lose. So I signed up.

On the day of the event, sweaty-palmed and shivering, I was handed a sheet containing subsets of the alphabet that had to be rearranged. This was the first time I had ever heard the word "anagram," and the first thing that I urgently wanted to rearrange was my decision to participate in this event. Since time travel was not an option, I took a deep breath and turned the page over to look at the questions.

To my surprise, random strings of gibberish came to life. One by one, the letters danced before my eyes and reordered themselves. I could see all permutations; as if by magic, the answers simply appeared. "AINOORT" became "ORATION," "CGINORS" became "SCORING." In the course of that one fateful hour, my life went from "WAOMESE" to "AWESOME." I breezed through the questions, and walked out leaving everyone bewildered—including myself.

From that point, there was no turning back. Now I was constantly on my Scrabble app, learning not only words but their etymologies and other nuances. I got involved in Scrabble quizzing and discovered it to be quite the team game:

> "I have another anagram for you: MOROUSIGN."
> "Wait, give me a minute."
> "I know this one! It's GINORMOUS, isn't it?"
> "Ginormous? What even is that? A nacho brand? Hey Siri, what does 'ginormous' mean?"
> *"OK, I found this on the web for 'what does Ghey Norm S mean.'"*

Our Scrabble practices often baffled Siri. But it was how we learned words. We were inquisitive, enthralled, consumed, inspired. Although GINORMOUS was not all that big a word, Scrabble came as a *ginormous* breakthrough for a child who could barely string two sentences together a short time before.

This was also how we learned context and application. It was a spontaneous process. The phobia I had carried within all those years dissolved, and with every game, my prowess blossomed—including my abilities *outside* the Scrabble board.

The true treasure at the heart of my Scrabble experience, however, was not my newfound conversance in a language that had eluded me throughout childhood (*nor* for that matter, the outstanding pleasure of defeating Shaurya in national Scrabble competitions), but rather an expansion of my intellectual vistas. Wittgenstein had highlighted the inextricable link between language and thought, and every time I converted "ANTIMUONS" to "MOUNTAINS," a new facet of the universe would open to me its grandeur. Out of a mere twenty-six letters, I could configure every object, concrete and abstract—every action, every quality...everything.

Summary

AH, ONE OF ATHENA'S CLASSICS. When Mehul arrived on Athena's shores, he was your standard strong "Indian Male STEM Applicant": competitive grades, competitive standardized tests scores, so-so extra-curricular activities. Like thousands of others. On top of that, he sought to apply for computer science, one of the most competitive programs at virtually every university. Blimey, what must we mentors do?

Thankfully, there was something else, a magic masala blend we could pour into the mix. Mehul had a quirk, one that was mentioned almost in passing during our first encounter: Scrabble. While most academically inclined scholars likely gravitated toward discussing a technical project in their Common Application Essay, Mehul leaned into this seemingly frivolous hobby, sharing its meaningful origins and how it transformed him from a shy lad to a mature, upstanding adolescent eager for bold undertakings. The result is a simple and artful story, delivered potently with a dash of style.

Values

ACTING DESPITE FEAR, PUSHING THROUGH WHEN the going gets tough, is the very definition of grit. The research of Angela Duckworth and other notable scholars highlights that grit is an essential quality for success, one that American culture—including its university system—especially prizes. Mehul feels insecure, Mehul gets knocked down, but he always gets back up and takes another shot. Grit is connected to another powerful concept, the growth mindset (coined by psychologist Carol Dweck). Without grit, without the capacity to persevere through discomfort, there can be no growth. Mehul implicitly embraces this ideal; he acknowledges his shortcomings, but believes that through concerted effort, he can transform himself and therefore his surroundings. Additionally, he's eager to broaden his knowledge—the "context and application" of language through Scrabble. *Nothing here screams computer science*, his intended area of study, for Mehul possesses the liberal arts mindset that elite universities like Stanford deeply cherish. He wants to understand big things, to expand his "intellectual vistas." On top of that, he embarks upon this process joyfully, bantering with his friends during friendly linguistic combat. Who said learning must be dull?

Perspective

THIS ESSAY IS REPLETE NOT ONLY with heart, but also with mind, with the "intellectual vitality" that Stanford explicitly wishes to see on campus. Mehul effectively underscores the academic insights he garners through his journey: for example, the importance of a word's connotations and the context in which it's employed. He also garners insights about himself: for example, discovering a knack for reordering letters to form words (please strive to uncover such skills in yourself—you never know!). Mehul further realizes that Scrabble can be a team game, which allows him to enrich his vocabulary and community simultaneously. He couples this awareness with a pleasant but powerful image of teens gathered in a circle playing word games for both linguistic development and recreation. After all, in addition to academic excellence, universities seek students who'll engage positively and productively with their peers, so this little image goes a long way!

And through the enjoyable tribulations of Scrabble, "[t]he phobia I had carried within all those years dissolved, and with every game my prowess blossomed—including my abilities *outside* the Scrabble board." Mehul goes on to quote the seminal philosopher Ludwig Wittgenstein, who isn't exactly a common reference in Indian youth circles, demonstrating the breadth of his reading and the expansive intellectual horizons toward which he sails. This essay isn't about Scrabble; it's about vanquishing self-limiting beliefs and remaking oneself continually into something more. And that, ladies and gentlemen, is the purpose of all education.

Authenticity

RIGHT OFF THE BAT, MEHUL IS unafraid to be vulnerable, recounting the embarrassing incident of a flight attendant laughing at his English peccadillo. Moreover, he unabashedly admits how the incident "gutted" him, resulting in his "berating [himself] for [his] incompetence with words." It's a distinctly human moment. The emotions elicited by this opening compel the reader to take Mehul's side (after all, everyone roots for the underdog). Vulnerability, as mentioned by UT Austin professor Brené Brown, is responsible for forging intense interpersonal bonds, including those between writers and readers!

The challenge of the so-called "Indian Male STEM Applicant" is to be open with one's audience. American readers have grown accustomed to seeing a style that feels detached and clinical, which results in a limited emotional connection. Not Mehul's, however. His authenticity beautifully re-emerges in later paragraphs. When he attends his first Scrabble competition, he's "sweaty-palmed and shivering," even admitting that "the first thing that I urgently wanted to rearrange was my decision to participate in this event." But he acts despite this fear, which reveals one of the values this young man cherishes. In addition, Mehul admits jealousy of his archrival, Shaurya, the "wordsmith of the class." Negative emotions are okay! They're *believable*. Everyone experiences envy, the green-eyed monster; Mehul's just courageous enough to acknowledge his own fallibility. We like him more as a result.

Craft

WHAT MAKES THE STORY COME TO life is Mehul's obvious command over the English language, which brilliantly subverts his supposed linguistic incompetence. The effect is genius, a sort of literary "humblebrag," if you will. Many word choices that Mehul employs are off the beaten trail, which further dissolves any concern that this young man is a charlatan. It's not every day that you see (an Indian techie) teenager incorporate "proverbial," "replete," "chasms," "flummoxed," and "laughingstock" into their work! There's also the statement, "I could never match his esoteric vocabulary and flowery turns of phrase," which is nothing if not ironic: Mehul's essay is full of esoteric vocabulary and flowery turns of phrase! He's a kid whose abiding love and passion for words feels palpable in every line.

Note also the consistent imagery that reappears intermittently, beginning with the "journey up the proverbial mountain" and culminating with the transformation of "ANTIMUONS" (a niche particle physics term, not gibberish!) to "MOUNTAINS." Such clever attention to aesthetic detail (the all-caps catch the reader's attention) is an additional flourish, which can really delight readers. But just to be clear that he's not a snobbish know-it-all, Mehul peppers his piece with pop culture references ("Word Muggle") and anagram-laden dialogues ("ginormous"). His willingness to have fun with language indicates a certain human warmth and relatability. Here's a scholar who can not only discuss the nuances of lexicography (the formal study of words), but also provide charmingly profound perspectives on the latest movie or TV show. He'll be an ideal student, peer, and friend at Stanford (a school that literally asks you to "write a note to your future roommate"!).

EXERCISE

Every hero has a rival. Who's yours? Do you consider yourselves enemies? Frenemies? Is it a healthy competition or something toxic? How has your rivalry evolved over time? Have you grown from the experience?

LAUGHING MATTERS: POLITICAL CHANGE ONE JOKE AT A TIME

ADITI DOGRA

Delhi-NCR

The University of Chicago

GROWING UP WITH THE TUTELAGE OF *Gilmore Girls*, I picked up wit. My wit was simply a mathematical function. Comedy = f(source material X). Often, this X was politics, a.k.a. the intellectual's reality show. Soon, my brain began to analyze everything for potential political references, generating witty rejoinders whenever possible. When my father asserted his daily dad joke, "A child is told to get ice, and she points a gun at the water and tells it to 'freeze!'"; I responded, "That is why we need gun control."

However, to my utter dismay, most of my peers considered me more a court jester than a court advisor, for my humor was not a "serious" hobby. What did a girl need to do to get some respect around here? That was when I found Shreya.

Shreya was Vice Head Girl.

Shreya was tall and thin and terrifyingly terrific.

Everyone - including I/me (not sure) - thought Shreya was so smart, so pretty, and so worthy of respect and admiration.

Shreya participated in Model UN.

I would participate in Model UN.

Given my previous knowledge of politics, MUN was not difficult, but a more solemn extracurricular activity existed not. I considered myself a Jane Austen character, restricted by corsets ("pantsuits") and the unnatural demands of society ("conduct in committee"). I liked politics, but when I proposed unorthodox solutions to solve problems sustainably, I gained no traction in a room of pantsuit-ed students regurgitating existing policy memos, eyeing only the "Best Delegate" certificate. There was pitifully little original analysis, and my brain, accustomed to independently evaluating and responding to every situation, remained deplorably unstimulated.

After such tragically comic events, I usually returned to comedy. On one such occasion, I watched John Oliver deliver a charmingly strident speech about tax evasion. The next day, casually surfing Twitter, I saw that he had canvassed 70,000 signatures to establish a church named Our Lady of Perpetual Exemption, a publicity stunt intended to demonstrate the ease of tax evasion.

This was my Eureka moment. Oliver's antics were not only hilarious; they also enlightened the public of a heretofore unrecognized problem and galvanized political change. Politics and comedy, far from polar opposites, were more "estranged siblings," more related than they cared to admit.

The landscape had changed: I was compelled not only to make jokes about current events, but also to create elaborate comedic content to inspire positive action of good against evil, like my heroes Oliver and Colbert. But what mischief might I make? One night, while watching *The Sound of Music*, Julie Andrews' blonde helmet (misplaced modifier, I know) bore strange resemblance to another iconic head of hair... and I imagined the Donald twirling around in a nightgown, singing his own rendition of "My Favorite Things." Things then spiraled pleasantly out of control, and I found myself spending weekends designing sets and recruiting my artistically talented peers to shoot satirical music videos targeting the issues that made me sad, mad, or (usually) both. I objectively evaluated the impact of my videos by the number of "views" they received on YouTube.

I found that my political satire helped my peers understand complex political issues and inspired them to participate in the political process, which can be a good thing in a democracy. When my peers watched my videos and laughed at my jokes, they also started to reflect on the socio-political ills in India, America, and around the world. This deeper engagement - along with laughter of course - was all the reward I needed. In the coming years, as I digest serious thoughts in hallowed halls, I will also refine this curious capability, and continue to harness it to enlighten my fellow men and women. Thanks for listening. Aditi, out.

Summary

WE NOW COME TO ONE OF the most entertaining essays you'll see! Aditi Dogra was certainly a character, quick-witted and eager to destroy any half-baked statement one might utter. Her flippant, incisive approach to English and Politics made her unique among a crowded, conservative pool of Indian STEM applicants. Therefore, when it came to the Common Application Essay, we certainly wished for Aditi to showcase her unique flair for comedic writing. But make no mistake! Pervading each line—intertwined with all the jabs—is profound introspection, revealing a thinker who'll undoubtedly raise the intellectual bar in any classroom or dining hall discussion.

Values

WHEN IT COMES TO VALUES, ADITI doesn't explicitly underscore them. She's too cool for that. Nevertheless, they naturally emerge as she recounts her tale. It's evident that this young lady cares about harnessing humor to highlight hypocrisies in public life worldwide, an essential step to building more enlightened societies. Aditi appreciates making complex concepts more accessible to others, especially those of her generation. And she achieves this feat through bold, unconventional styles of communication, such as her Donald Trump rendition of "My Favorite Things."

Moreover, Aditi cares deeply about discovering herself, her purpose, her work. Sincerity is always in high demand and short supply. With this author, we see a girl who's open to everything, but who'll also evaluate whether an activity resonates with her talents and passions. Hence, despite feeling the pressure to dive into MUN, she soon recognizes the shortcomings of the organization's traditional events, which can sometimes be mired in protocol and lack vibrant, substantive debates. And so, she leaves it. She has no qualms about fitting into existing molds; rather, she investigates whether each endeavor possesses the capacity to captivate her. This combination of genuine openness and critical evaluation is rare. It's the mark of a mature mind capable of thinking for itself and making important life decisions. After all, American universities like UChicago seek to be bastions of free thought—they want to see diversity in all its forms, not just race and ethnicity!

Perspective

THERE ARE MULTIPLE HARD-HITTING INSIGHTS THROUGHOUT this piece. The first we categorize as a "Synthesis" insight: A and B aren't mutually exclusive, and in fact can co-exist in elegant harmony. In Aditi's case, the synthesis helps reconcile an internal battle that'd been raging: "Politics and comedy, far from polar opposites, were more 'estranged siblings,'" more related than they cared to admit." Again, as we see with other essays, the capacity to forge connections between disparate disciplines and fields is a cornerstone of the liberal arts mindset, one that US universities in particular wish to observe and cultivate in their budding scholars.

Building off the above, Aditi's secondary insight is that she possesses the gift of creating comedic content to inspire positive action of good against evil, just like her media heroes. And when she discovers this superpower, we can't help but feel that we're witnessing a Marvel origin story. The formerly shy high schooler is now ready to wield the weapon of satire in her quest for a saner world.

Authenticity

"THE WEAK SHOWS HIS STRENGTH AND hides his weaknesses; the magnificent exhibits his weaknesses like ornaments." Nassim Taleb's quote is one of our favorites. And in its spirit, Aditi parades her flaws like they're the newest additions to Milan Fashion Week, lamenting that "most of my peers considered me more a court jester than a court advisor." She also doesn't pretend to have selfless reasons for joining MUN, unabashedly admitting that she just wanted to be more like

Shreya. Also check out all the quirky parenthetical one-liners, which convey an honesty that few authors permit for themselves: "Everyone-including I/me (not sure)...One night, while watching The *Sound of Music,* Julie Andrews' blonde helmet (misplaced modifier, I know) bore strange resemblance..."

Again, feigning strength is weak. It's like another quote from bestselling author Jesus Christ: "Those who exalt themselves are humbled; those who humble themselves are exalted." So humble yourselves, kids.

Craft

AS A LITERATURE APPLICANT, ADITI CERTAINLY had a way with words, but we can assure you that she arrived at this final product only after eight drafts. There's no glory without grind.

And this is no doubt a glorious essay. But how did Aditi achieve its effect? Well, here again we see a curious, charming juxtaposition of intellect and humor. The diction—from "idiocy, debauchery and (occasional) decency" to "deplorably unstimulated"—is beyond the range of a typical 17-year-old's. Immediately, it signals to the reader that we're dealing with a rather precocious gal. When we blend this competence with humor throughout the piece, we start imagining Aditi as a future host of *The Daily Show*, sharing her satire with young audiences around the globe.

We want to delve deeper into the uniqueness of the humor demonstrated in this essay. It sometimes emerges so subtly, so smoothly (the tutelage of *Gilmore Girls*); on other occasions, it's daring, even brazen. Again, have you ever seen an application essay in which a student makes a grammatical mistake, then shrugs it off, essentially stating that she's too busy (or rather, too interesting) to belabor such trivial matters? Now, she can get away with this apparent *faux pas* because she demonstrates, without a shred of doubt, that her command over the English language is irreproachable. If only more Indian students understood concepts like misplaced modifiers, the average SAT score might just shoot up!

Another note on craft: we love the changing tones. We have traditional sentences, as well as a pseudo-mathematical equation ("Comedy = f(source material X)") and a sudden outburst that's perfectly in character ("What did a girl need to do to get some respect around here?!"), replete with a double punctuation mark. These choices, like the author, are not for the faint of heart…

EXERCISE

What makes you insecure? Can you discuss that insecurity in the third person, adding an element of humor to the mix?

The Dichotomy of Perception: Dissecting the Dualism of Science and Art

AASTHA TIWARI

Delhi-NCR

Princeton University

Abstract

IN THE FOLLOWING RESEARCH PAPER, Aastha Tiwari embarks on a daring intellectual experiment to dissect one of the most vexing conundrums that has plagued human thought: the relationship between science and art. Her conclusion, much to her own surprise (and that of the entire scientific community of her household), ran counter to popular opinion. Read on, dear Sir or Madam.

Hypothesis

MS. TIWARI'S INITIAL ASSUMPTION WAS THAT scientific principles and methods enhanced the pursuit of the arts, and that those of the arts did likewise for the sciences. Despite hearing it repeatedly in cocktail parties, this hypothesis had increasingly rendered Ms. Tiwari a tad uneasy, for reasons "easier felt than expressed." Therefore, she (in characteristic style) insisted on testing the assumption that science and art fundamentally overlap, before incorporating it as a pillar of her guiding philosophy.

Methods and Procedure

THE FOLLOWING EXPERIMENT WAS DESIGNED TO test which philosophical perspective on the relationship between science and art was more "productive" (for this was the variable Ms. Tiwari chose to optimize). Must she consider science and art together, as supplements, or conduct scientific and artistic endeavors separately? Ms. Tiwari was asked to complete several tasks segregated into three setups labeled: Test Group, Control 1, and Control 2. The following is a brief outline of each experimental setup.

Test Group

THIS SETUP WAS DEDICATED TO MEASURING Ms. Tiwari's productivity in science and art when performed simultaneously. She was instructed to hold both scientific and artistic paradigms in her mind at the same time, for example, by pondering the chemical properties of the different paints she employed to paint a portrait. In similar fashion, she reveled in the aesthetic appeal of her solar-powered air ionizer while designing it. Oooh. Her output was documented through her work at various scientific competitions and art exhibitions.

Control 1

THE SECOND SETUP WAS DESIGNED TO measure Ms. Tiwari's performance in a purely artistic framework. This implied that she was NOT to contemplate the mathematics of the golden ratio while painting flowers, and instead to simply paint flowers; she was NOT to force symmetry onto her landscapes, and simply paint what she imagined. Her deliverable was presented in the form of another art exhibition.

Control 2

THE THIRD SETUP WAS DEDICATED TO measuring her output in the realm of the pure sciences. She was often found basking in the warmth of catalytic oxidation mechanisms, lazily reading *Biochemistry* (Stryer), and laughing uncontrollably at certain science puns. She submitted a deliverable through her work on a micro-drone, patent pending, and her efforts to woo juniors to her beloved Science Society.

Results

THE QUANTITY AND QUALITY OF OUTPUT in all three setups was measured and adjusted for time. The results were staggering.

In Ms. Tiwari's case, pondering science and art separately resulted in greater progress than combining the paradigms.

Conclusion

MS. TIWARI SUBCONSCIOUSLY UNDERSTANDS A MAJOR difference between science and art. Science, to her, is about perceiving reality the way it is; art is about perceiving reality the way it can be. One demonstrates realism, the other, idealism. Often, Aastha dons the hat of scientist, and meticulously dissects the world to unravel causal mechanisms. Through the Control 2 setup, she avoided many a logical fallacy, as she was not fixed to preconceived patterns. But through Control 1, Aastha adopted a different operating system, imagining what is not there, and manifesting that vision through a variety of aesthetic media, unconstrained by the laws of physics or material possibility.

Both are powerful. But both are distinct, and she has arrived at the conclusion that she will keep it that way, unless follow-up experiments and/or conversations with peers and professors provide conclusive evidence to the contrary. But for now, her intellectual philosophy is defined by this dualism. She will continue to love both art and science, similarly but separately.

As Ms. Tiwari often quips, it takes discipline (on occasion) not to be interdisciplinary.

Summary

WE MUST ADMIT, AASTHA INITIALLY CLASHED with her Athena mentors, given that everyone in the mix was rather headstrong. However, with time, a mutual respect emerged, as we came to understand what made this truly unique teenager tick. While ideating Aastha's essay, in our pursuit of perfection, we kept hitting roadblocks. Exasperated, she finally uttered, "Why can't I just write a research paper? That would be so much simpler!" After all, Aastha was the quintessential scholar, with numerous academic articles already to her name. She ate, drank, and breathed the scientific method; she'd been experimenting and tinkering since she was a toddler. Therefore, her outburst gave us pause. The rest is history.

Values

LET'S NEVER FORGET THE CORE VALUES of any elite educational institution. The Princetons of the world serve as self-designated repositories of humankind's wisdom, and strive to build on that foundation into the future. This applies from physics, to politics, to philosophy. Naturally, when they see a young person come along who genuinely, with every fiber of their being, wishes to pursue a "life of the mind" and uncover the universe's secrets, they lean in and listen closer. Aastha's "intellectual vitality," or desire to attain knowledge for its own sake—not merely as a means to obtain wealth or status—is therefore most appreciated.

But, this isn't all! The Ivy Leagues and their peers have their roots in the educational philosophy of Ancient Greece (and to a lesser extent, Rome). The stalwarts of the time were synthetic thinkers, uniting insights from a diverse array of disciplines, from mathematics to gymnastics (the Greeks were intent on physical fitness, hence the Olympics). This "liberal arts" mindset was reinforced during the Renaissance, when Da Vinci, Michaelangelo, and their contemporaries painstakingly refined their abilities in both art and science. The "Renaissance Man" came to symbolize a creative individual whose intellectual and practical skills transcended limited domains, one who could harness all parts of their brain to think, solve problems, and produce masterpieces that survive to this day. Even now, centuries later, colleges glorify the same ideal, the same aspiration in the candidates who join their ranks. And from what we see here, Aastha Tiwari fits the bill!

Perspective

THE CROWNING JEWEL OF THE ESSAY. The seemingly unintuitive conclusion. Most well-intentioned thinkers (like the author herself, initially) might subscribe to the convenient, even simplistic assumption that the arts and sciences are similar. But Aastha adopts a more nuanced view, that there in fact exists an unbridgeable chasm between the two. Not only do the twain not meet; they must not meet! For they fulfill two very different human impulses: the desire for understanding and the desire for creativity. In the former, the world is constant, and we are variable; in the latter, the roles are flipped. Attempting to do both simultaneously results only in muddiness, sloppiness. No serious scholar can accept that.

So with this profound touch, you have a piece that checks off every box by thinking way outside the box. The lesson isn't to imitate the form or even the content; it's to find your own form and content, your own voice, the story only you can tell. This is the case in college admissions, in the professional world, and in life itself.

Authenticity

IT KEEPS RESURFACING: DON'T BE AFRAID to be unapologetically yourself. By owning her nerdiness—with self-effacing comedy—Aastha develops a distinct swagger that the reader can't help but find charming. Just note all the dry, deadpan wit in lines like, "Her conclusion, much to her own surprise (and that of the entire scientific community of her household)" or "Oooh." Her self-deprecation keeps her choice of third-person perspective from appearing detached or impersonal, unlike an actual scientific paper! She laughs uncontrollably at science puns and struggles to woo her juniors to join her beloved Science Society. She proposes a "hypothesis" with great confidence and finds herself humbled when it's proven wrong. And by embodying this fearlessness, she signals confidence, even strength. That's the irony: in puffing ourselves up, we appear weak. In unabashedly showcasing our weaknesses, we appear (and become) stronger.

Craft

THE MEEK SHALL INHERIT THE EARTH, but so shall the bold! Life advice that has served us well: when it's between playing it safe and experimenting with novelty, choose the latter. Guided by this mantra, we decided to proceed with this daring structure: Athena's only Common Application Essay in the form of a mock academic paper.

However, this structure didn't emerge out of the blue. Given Aastha's interest in the pure sciences (she's definitely more Sheldon than Howard), the form also highlights her dedication to the pursuit and production of knowledge, the hallmark of any budding scholar.

And this point, we wish to emphasize: stylistic embellishments by themselves hold little value. Writing an essay in the form of a script does little unless screenwriting is an integral element of an applicant's profile; otherwise, it's but a gimmick that can backfire as a half-baked attempt to earn brownie points. *Authenticity, authenticity, authenticity.*

But that's not all. What makes this fun parody come to life is the juxtaposition of the research paper form with humorous content. The alternating formal and informal tones delight the reader; the utterly distinct literary voice highlights a personality trait AOs may not expect from an Indian girl in STEM. Moreover, Aastha refers to herself in the third-person throughout. Again, this is on brand: here's a young lady who seeks to examine herself—her thoughts, her feelings, her values— with the same objectivity she brings to pipetting *E. coli* onto a petri dish. This is the level of thought invested into each stylistic choice. "The medium is the message," goes Marshall McLuhan's famous marketing adage. Aastha has something to say and a meaningful way to say it; the two are inextricable...

EXERCISE

Consider a hypothesis or assumption about any topic. How would you investigate its veracity? Can you identify the steps necessary to arriving at a convincing conclusion? What would your evidence be?

Laughter as Liberation: Navigating Prejudice with Humor

YASH KHATRI

Delhi-NCR

Brown University

GROWING UP AS A SIKH IN post-9/11 United States was tough. A sixth grader is usually expected to solve linear equations or create dioramas of the Amazon rainforest - not deal with daily microaggressions. I was called a "terrorist," a "towel head," and Osama Bin Laden's relative. At eleven, I barely understood these racist terms; however, I understood that I was unwelcome.

I first endeavored to instruct my peers that not all men with beards were Muslim. There were also Sikhs, Orthodox Jews, Hindu Swamis, Jesus Christ, and Zach Galifianakis. Like Americans of all faiths, Sikhs were appalled by the events of 9/11.

But sixth graders are rarely receptive to lessons in the sociology of religion. What else could I do? Involve my parents? Write to President Obama? Launch a revolution? Start a Fight Club? Given the size of my tormentors, I did not like my odds.

As the great Harvey Specter stated, there is always another option. One day, a classmate jeered, for the tenth time, "How was dinner with Bin Laden last night?" Too exhausted for anger, I responded, "Oh, it was the bomb!" Laughter erupted. Looking up, I was astonished to realize that, for the first time, my classmates were laughing *with* me, not *at* me.

I most certainly did not see this coming. While historical facts fell on deaf ears, a joke penetrated the "veil of ignorance" and elevated the mood.

Gradually, as my jokes diffused to other arenas of my life, I grew to appreciate their versatility and power. During a session of the UN Security Council, the Russian delegate insisted on Russia's claim to the Crimean Peninsula. Exasperated, I intervened: "Are we really going to trust a country that eats states like it's playing Hungry Hungry Hippos?!" This transformed the energy of the room, allowing the other delegates to voice their opinions against the strident Russian, who was now half-smiling and open to reason. Through a subtle combination of humor, which got people laughing, and critique, which got people thinking, I was able to steer the discussion to a consensus. I had discovered a powerful tool for diplomacy, for avoiding antagonism and facilitating collaboration.

I increasingly realized that by continually refining humor, I developed a capacity to influence others to positive outcomes. It worked on a personal level, as well as in a group. But could I use humor to address socio-political injustices close to my heart? Given my childhood brush with racism, I was extremely sensitive to inequality, and disheartened by its ubiquity in my immediate environment. I wanted to intentionally galvanize systemic change.

Humor has become a part of me, and I use it to navigate a range of situations. It is an effective defense mechanism, it diffuses conflicts, and it is a potent tool to raise public awareness and motivate transformative action. Used skillfully, humor instantaneously diminishes the power of the oppressor and empowers the formerly oppressed. We as a society must use this and other inventive methods to promote social justice. Textbooks are important, but satire is often the sugar that helps the medicine go down. As I struggle to continue to promote liberal ideals like multiculturalism, I will keep the weapon of humor in my arsenal.

Summary

ONE OF THE CARDINAL RULES OF screenwriting is that the hero is only as strong as the villain allows them to be. The more we fear the Joker, the more we appreciate Batman. Harry Potter's ultimate victory over Voldemort is all the sweeter given that the entire wizarding word is terrified of uttering the latter's name. If you want to tell a story of triumph, you must first establish the "credentials" of the obstacle. And that's precisely how Yash's essay begins. Being a member of a minority religious group gave this US-based student a diversity hook within the Indian American community. But truly, it was his distinct struggle against the enemy of mistaken discrimination that made him a compelling character to meet.

Values

LET'S START WITH THE VALUES YASH reveals. There are many. Firstly, here's a young man never afraid to stick up for the underdog, given that he's been marginalized himself, and thus wants to save others from similar plights. We want to emphasize the powerful union of micro and macro, the fact that the same principle Yash discovers is applicable on a societal scale to address historical injustices. And he not only recognizes that reality intellectually, but also grabs his microphone and starts roaming the streets of Delhi, getting his compatriots to think and feel more—the first steps to "galvaniz[ing] systemic change." This narrative even resembles the arcs of most superhero movies: the protagonist first learns to defend themselves, and then realizes that their powers must be leveraged for something greater, a philosophical ideal. It's this dedication to a cause that makes us root for them, not their supernatural abilities.

An important point to note is that the college Yash ultimately attended embraces similar values. Brown is big on multiculturalism and social justice, so a young man who embraces his identity when others don't, and who fights for unheard voices, is exactly the type of scholar and leader they wish to invest in: a brand ambassador who'll make them proud for decades to come.

Perspective

AS WE SEE WITH COUNTLESS SUPERHEROES, these early struggles compel them to develop powers beyond the realm of the ordinary.

And for Yash, this happens the very moment he responds to his tormentors with a timely joke ("It was the bomb!"). At that moment, he recounts his dawning realization, the driving thrust of the entire piece: through humor, he can get others to laugh *with* him, not *at* him. He then takes it further during the MUN competitions ("Hungry Hungry Hippos!") and continues to refine his new craft into a formidable tool to defend himself.

What lends this essay an added dimension is that connection between micro and macro. Yash contextualizes his experience within a broader socio-political context, highlighting that humor is a powerful tool in the arsenal of the oppressed, especially when you're attempting to overturn an entrenched perspective: "While historical facts fell on deaf ears, a joke penetrated the 'veil of ignorance' and elevated the mood."

But there are layers to this insight. Humor not only imparts novel perspectives, but also makes others more receptive to future critiques, getting them to open their hearts and minds. And Yash recognizes how essential this tool is for diplomacy, whether between people or between nations. Plus, it proved additionally helpful, given that he ended up applying for (and majoring in) politics! This metatheme is driven home crisply and comprehensively in the conclusion: "Humor has become a part of me, and I use it to navigate a range of situations. It is an effective defense mechanism, it diffuses conflicts, and it is a potent tool to raise public awareness and to motivate transformative action."

Authenticity

IN THE VERY FIRST PARAGRAPH, THE author musters the courage to face his tormentors, sharing details of his ordeals growing up Sikh in post-9/11 America, where he was routinely called a "terrorist," a "towel head," and "Osama bin Laden's relative." Here, we want to emphasize that the specifics bring this otherwise standard bullying-essay narrative to life. Yash could simply have stated that he was mistreated as a child. But that would have fallen flat! Including the context, especially the explicit terms he faced on a daily basis, places the reader in his shoes, allowing us to partly experience the challenges of wandering an American hallway with a turban. Don't be afraid to tell your story in detail. Readers connect when you paint the full picture, not just the broad strokes.

Craft

Now, the final nail in the coffin. However great the story, it wouldn't have clicked unless Yash walked the walk, demonstrating his humor in the writing itself. A show equals a thousand tells. For example, one of our favorites is "[S]ixth graders are rarely receptive to lessons in the sociology of religion." The juxtaposition of elementary-school students and a complex, multidisciplinary subject like the sociology of religion is immediately comical, and the phraseology reveals the author's intellectual maturity. He does something similar by mentioning Jesus Christ and Zach Galifianakis in the same sentence—which to our knowledge, has never been done before. And it's not just once or twice; the witty allusions are peppered throughout the paragraphs, from *Fight Club* to Harvey Specter. As a result, we have a heartwarming hero's journey, a fearless young man who has revealed to admissions officers the many ways he'll enrich his peers on campus. And that, he certainly did.

EXERCISE

Take a serious activity you do (statistical research, Indian classical dance) and discuss it in a lighthearted manner. Or take a frivolous activity (playing video games, doom-scrolling Instagram) and discuss it seriously. Can you convince your reader to see your point of view?

ECHOES OF THE ZENANA: VOICES IN THE ART

NAVYA AGARWAL

Bangalore

Stanford University

COLD, HARD MARBLE PRESSED AGAINST MY paint-splattered legs as I pored over my near-finished painting. It was 3 AM, and the sari-clad, pot-carrying woman on my canvas stared back at me.

As I swirled my brush in murky turpentine, the posters lining my bedroom wall seemed to speak. A scene of suffragettes marching. *GRL PWR. Young people can change the world.* Adorned with messages of changemakers throughout history, my walls held a mirror to my mission, the impact I longed to make. Yet, by painting portraits alone in my room, what did I stand to change?

The question lingered like paint on my fingertips, accompanying me on my annual visit to my grandparents in Jaipur.

★★★

ASCENDING THE WINDING STAIRCASE OF JAIPUR'S Pink Palace, I entered the Zenana, the women's chambers. Peering through the same ornate windows that generations of women had before me, I imagined my ancestors maintaining purdah, a tradition designed to veil women from public view. The room's intricate latticework ensured one could

32

see out, but no one could see in. Today, the Zenana remains the only vestige of Jaipur's captive women, its walls alive with the whispers of those erased from history's pages.

Beautiful, isn't it?

I leaned into the sandstone, just barely discerning a faint symphony of voices.

We spent our lives here, but it was never ours. The Prince of Jaipur commissioned it to confine us, his concubines. It holds our stories, but we couldn't tell them.

The thrum of my pulse beat in sync with the lilting sound, as though we were one.

We never had a say in the spaces we tread. In the legacy we left.

Deep beneath Jaipur's domed canopies and fluted pillars echoed the murmurs of protagonists whose narratives were authored by their oppressors. Their fate was set in stone.

A rush of urgency coursed through me. The portraits I painted seemed empowering, but really, I was not so different from the architect of the Zenana—narrating stories not mine to tell.

As my concept of storytelling evolved, so, too, did my art.

WHEN I RETURNED HOME TO MY city, I sought guidance from a prominent activist. Sitting across from her, I listened, enraptured, as she relayed her experiences in service. Stories—genuine, heart-wrenching stories—streamed forth, until suddenly, she hesitated.

"What is it?" I asked.

"I'm not sure you'll be comfortable with this one. Shall I stop?"

My wide eyes betrayed my unbridled curiosity. She told me about young sex-trafficking survivors living in a home hidden from society's eyes.

A WEEK LATER, THERE I STOOD. Looking around me, I saw girls not so dissimilar from the women of Jaipur, each brimming with stories—personal, vulnerable, authentic—waiting to be shared.

A vast white wall towered before us. One by one, the girls stepped forward and splattered paint with unfettered abandon. Their pasts had been shrouded by shame. Now, art became their medium to speak for themselves, with absolute, uncompromising honesty.

I stepped back. The once-somber room fluttered to life with a kaleidoscope of butterflies—magenta, violet, indigo—each a symbol of metamorphosis. It was as if the girls had emerged from the chrysalises of their pasts and rejoiced in the unfolding of catharsis. *This* was the impact I had always sought: a transformation far bigger than myself.

"*Didi,* this mural will be here forever!" one girl exclaimed.

It dawned on me that although the colors may fade, the girls' voices would endure. The mural was a monument that belonged to them, designed by them.

FOUR YEARS AND SIXTEEN MURALS LATER, I know that to empower the narratives of others, I must pass them the paintbrush. As I help create space for the marginalized, I must ensure that history paints a more inclusive and genuine portrait of my community's rich mosaic.

In the powerful mural of humanity, I hope to contribute some color, so that my ancestors have not been silenced in vain.

Summary

THIS IS ONE CAE THAT FITS squarely into the much-maligned genre we call the "Project Essay." When done poorly, a Project Essay—that is, a CAE written about one's extracurricular project—can read like a hollow, formulaic expansion of one's resume. Hence, Project Essays get a bad rep for being lazy or basic. When done right, however, they can highlight facets of one's experience that far transcend the Activity List.

That's what we have here. Since Navya possessed what we call a "Leadership/Service" profile—a resume centered around assuming leadership positions and producing positive impact on others—it only made sense to showcase it. She'd achieved a number of impressive accomplishments for her work in a niche domain, the empowerment of local women through art, so discussing these themes was a no-brainer. The only challenge was execution: how to convey her message? We settled on a layered narrative essay that portrayed two of Navya's primary academic interests, history and art (primarily of South Asia), in a parallel manner. Our goal was to capture the inspirational, compassionate young changemaker Navya was, but also the distinct self-awareness that allowed her to transcend such a potentially superficial, goody two-shoes image. In the end, that very self-awareness, a rare commodity for high schoolers, was what made her distinct and intriguing among other students within her demographic of affluent, Indian American, female third-culture kids with non-STEM inclinations.

Values

MOST HIGH- SCHOOL STUDENTS DON'T REALLY know who they are or what they care about. (Heck, most adults probably don't even know either!) Navya wasn't one of them. From the start, it was clear that this girl was on a *mission*. All of her projects demonstrated a clear concern for others, which drew her to spearhead initiatives like a mural project involving young women who'd suffered abuse. Her rare, genuine desire to make the world a better place resonated with universities' missions to do the same.

As early as the second paragraph, it's clear that this girl wants to do great things. How could you not want to support such dreams, especially when they're directed toward her own community? See, instead of being a broad, detached altruist, wishing to help the globe at large, Navya cares specifically about her people. She regularly visits her family in Jaipur and seeks to help fellow Indian women she identifies as her "ancestors." Later, she aids fellow Indian women who've suffered trauma and disadvantages that she herself has not; hearing about their plight brings her to an emotional moment...and to action. Such traits are all the rage at elite American universities these days, for they reflect an idea we like to call "Cultural Rootedness," or being aware of one's own heritage. Having a specific niche helps make a student appear more genuine and diverse. After all, any kid can try to save the world. But as they say, "charity starts at home." You have to think global and act local.

Perspective

OF COURSE, NAVYA'S HEARTFELT CONCERN FOR women's empowerment would've been just satisfactory had she stopped there. Colleges love kids who represent the Next Generation of Leaders (™). But you know the problem with many of those kids? They're boring! Readers need to know how you think, not just what you do. They need to understand the *why*. Within the "Project Essay" genre, there's a sub-genre we like to call the "Do-Gooder Essay." Navya avoided its pitfalls by demonstrating intellectual and emotional maturity. What we noticed foremost about her was a deep-seated capacity for what psychology experts call "mentalization," or the ability to imagine how others think and feel. Young children lack this skill until they've been fully socialized by the adult world. (Unfortunately, many adults still never develop it!) Throughout the essay, she tries picturing—or better, hearing—the experiences of ancient women in her homeland. She presents their frustrations with being hidden away, made invisible by the men in power. Yes, Navya is astute to recognize that patriarchy was a form of systemic oppression with a distinct context, her ancestral city of Jaipur. She uses the Zenana as a symbol of its cruelty, and then offers reflections on how similar problems affect sexually abused Indian women today, themselves rendered silent, just without fancy windows to peer through. Few writers her age would manage to identify the women as "protagonists whose narratives were authored by their oppressors." It's a nuance that pays off later when we learn more about her character.

Authenticity

OCCASIONALLY, PERSPECTIVE AND AUTHENTICITY ARE ONE and the same in an essay. That's a good thing! In this narrative, the Pivot—or epiphany—occurs relatively early, at the point when Navya experiences a pivotal realization: "The portraits I painted seemed empowering, but really, I was not so different from the architect of the Zenana— narrating stories not mine to tell." This moment is what AOs like to call "self-implication." It's uncommon to see in application essays because kids are typically taught to portray themselves as perfect throughout their applications. Admitting flaws or faults seems to violate the cardinal rule of criminal law: never admit guilt!

Fortunately, this isn't law. The college admissions community is constantly seeking students who can critique themselves, perhaps even laugh about it. Now, Navya is no humorist in this essay, but she's not taking herself too seriously, either. The most believable people, paradoxically, are those who can engage in a bit of self-deprecation.

Acknowledging that she herself is a part of the problem is a sophisticated move. It reflects someone who hasn't let themselves fall into the savior complex that ensnares so many other self-righteous Do-Gooders. When you're already an affluent applicant who hasn't suffered the social ills of poverty or oppression, no one wants to hear you pontificate about how good a person you are. Instead, they want to see whether you have layers: nuance, complexity, self-awareness, historical context, artistic activism.

The fundamental question is: are you willing to be imperfect and strive toward being better? If so, lean into that.

Craft

SOME ESSAYS ARE SHOWY AND ORNATE in a literary way, but that sort of style didn't really fit Navya, or at least her story. The whole idea was about subtlety. Structurally, on the surface, you have a somewhat disjointed narrative, punctuated by seemingly separate vignettes. Deeper, you have two primary narratives, running in parallel, with an initial setup that establishes the problem our author faces: how to foster positive social impact through art? Our theme here is a central image, a central idea—that of silencing. Navya's "ancestors" were silenced by powerful men, just as her sex-trafficked peers were by society—but at the same time, Navya herself was the one silencing women by painting works for them instead of *with* them.

Note how the "silencing" idea manifests in distinct phrasings throughout the essay that play with the extended metaphor ("faint symphony of voices," "speak for themselves"). Every word choice feels deliberate, especially in the passages about the Zenana. This is a student who clearly cares about history and art (her intended areas of study), as evidenced by all the niche word choices like *purdah* and *latticework*, many of which will be foreign to a typical American reader. There's a distinct love here, a love for the world around her, past and present—"agape," as the Greeks called it. And as Oprah Winfrey says, love is in the details.

EXERCISE

Have there been any times when you found that YOU were part of the problem? (For example: a social issue, a group effort, etc.) What was your role, and what did you do about it?

From Himalayan Foothills to Hallowed Halls: A Journey of Determination

AAMISH AHMAD BEG

Lucknow

Dartmouth College

1998. A LONE FIGURE IN A crowded train compartment. An arduous journey from the foothills of the Himalayas to the riverbanks of the Ganges. Offer letter clutched tight, Akhlak Ahmad made his way to the hallowed halls of the Indian Institute of Technology, IIT, his one ticket to salvation.

My father was a glimmer of hope for us Nepali Muslims, a community pushed to the country's margins. He liberated himself from abject poverty through the fateful Joint Entrance Examination, the JEE, administered by India's government to decide the select few who would study at its finest institutions. Each year, millions seek the same liberation through the requisite single-minded process of preparation. My turn was next.

Confining myself to a single room, I repeated the same sums and pored over the same textbooks for years. Beyond those four walls, I could hear the growing crescendo of expectation. "Son of Indo-Nepali hope, destined to tread the same path his father tread"—the *only* path there was.

JEE PREP BOOKS LAY OPEN BESIDE an empty chair.

I was scraping together neural-nets to gauge Twitter's sentiment toward the game *Fallout* (spoiler alert: not great). With every command I typed, the circuits in my brain sparked to life, lines of bytes flowing before me. As I conjured code in earnest concentration, all else quieted into silence.

Awaking from my trance, I returned hesitantly to the thick books—sums half-finished, dreams half-fulfilled.

9TH GRADE. AN INVITATION TO JOIN the only high-school team attending Techniche: IIT Guwahati's college-level international tech fest. My test date was a week away. Error messages arose like pop-ups in my brain.

> **Warning:** *Divergence from your predetermined path.*
> **Error 404:** *Secure future for your family not found.*
> **Caution:** *Papa's hard work going to waste.*

Could I really do this?

★ ★ ★

2018. A FLIGHT FROM THE ORDERED roads of Lucknow to the winding roads of Guwahati. A boy, 800 miles from home, prepared to challenge his destiny.

From the outset, Techniche wasn't just a "tech fest;" it was a breeding ground for invention, the confluence of diverse disciplines—a hub of joyful learning.

As I strolled past booths teeming with water-powered engines, silk-based lung transplants, and other artifacts born of pure innovation, I felt *truly* educated. No preparatory textbooks or prescribed syllabi. No rote memorization. No monotony.

On the seventh day came my hour of reckoning: the General Championship, the culmination of a week spent in the lap of ingenuity.

My mind raced, waves of anxiety surging through my axons. The opposition comprised dozens of teams, all eager to claim glory.

As I gripped my borrowed laptop, ready to begin, I realized it lacked the required software. Whipping out a terminal session, I instantiated a makeshift Anaconda environment, retrieved the required packages, and got going.

Confidence (and code) streaming through me, I created an accurate regressor in under fifteen minutes. In that moment, I was back in my Himalayan village, filled with a curious calm.

I'd won.

The coveted golden trophy felt light in my hands, like the burden I had been carrying. Slowly, error windows closed, (copper) wires straightened, and it became clear that the future was my choice.

Gazing out into the crowd, I saw a young Akhlak. He nodded.

I felt a familiar tug of responsibility, but this time was different. I bore a duty not only to my father but also to myself. While our paths diverged, our shared spirit of boldness endured. He took a chance then. I was now.

Soon after, I launched a year-long app development bootcamp for students across Lucknow, determined to present creative paths for others like me. That an IIT inspired it is not lost on us, rather welcome.

★ ★ ★

2022. AN 18-HOUR FLIGHT DEPARTS FROM the world's largest democracy to its oldest. Shiny new passport clutched tight, a budding tech educator approaches the hallowed halls of American education: a *different* Indo-Nepali hope.

Summary

INDO-NEPALI BACKGROUND. MUSLIM. MODEST INCOME. FEW international applicants occupy so many in-demand demographic baskets. Aamish's interest in computer science and entrepreneurship was far more common among Indian males, of course, but it was the combination of factors that gave him a potential hook. Here was a kid who genuinely wished to emulate his heroic father, who'd overcome great challenges to achieve relative success…but what made Aamish interesting was his willingness to critique that idea, to interrogate it. He could've easily become an unthinking devotee who idolized a parent, only he made the conscious decision not to. Why? We wanted to know more. Hence, we had him write what is ostensibly a Project/Do-Gooder Essay that functions more like a parallel origin story. This is the making of an ambitious young man's journey. You want to feel inspired. You want to know what comes next!

Values

IT WAS ALWAYS CLEAR THAT AAMISH was a leader, but not necessarily in the typical student council president or sports captain sort of way. Instead, he represented leadership in its most fundamental sense, the soul of any true entrepreneur: a willingness to take risks, be different, and forge one's own path. The altruism he demonstrated through his wish to help others—"Soon after, I launched a year-long app development bootcamp for students across Lucknow, determined to present creative paths for others like me"—allowed him to burst his own egocentric bubble.

So many candidates get so lost in their personal narratives that they fail to become someone we can all wish to follow. Aamish, in contrast, wants to do big things for his community (Cultural Rootedness). He wants to make everyone proud. Leadership is a responsibility he willingly assumes—albeit with a twist. Similar to Aditi, he's unafraid to possess strong opinions. He explicitly disagrees with the Indian education system's philosophy ("I repeated the same sums and pored over the same textbooks for years"). That sort of "boldness" is what American universities love—within reason. Too much, and you can appear negative, even spiteful (a clear red flag!). Thankfully, Aamish toes the line by avoiding derogatory word choices ("requisite single-minded process of preparation" instead of his earlier drafts' "mechanical, repetitive, and single-minded labor.") He keeps focused on the positive, his newfound passion: "With every command I typed, the circuits in my brain sparked to life, lines of bytes flowing before me." The result is an Indian techpreneurship-oriented male in love with the liberal arts mindset of the American tradition. Catnip to AOs' ears!

And, of course, none of this would've been so compelling had Aamish not played into his ethnic/national/religious minority ancestry. By branding himself the "Indo-Nepali hope," he carves out a niche for himself as a champion of his (underrepresented) people. Marginalized by society, his father made the most of his circumstances, and by extension, so has Aamish with his own. Wouldn't you want to support someone with such lofty aspirations?

Perspective

WHEN THE PIVOT ARISES, AAMISH DOES something that elevates his narrative far beyond the standard Do-Gooder Essay plot: he develops nuance. Most kids aren't yet mature enough to do so. Where he could've simply ended things at "I'd won," he instead offers a whole concluding discussion of how "it became clear that the future was my choice." The individualism of American society often portrays the East as "collectivist," so Aamish resonates with Western ideas of maturity as synonymous with autonomy. Seeing an author achieve true intellectual and emotional independence is nothing if not assuring:

> I felt a familiar tug of responsibility, but this time was different. I bore a duty not only to my father but also to myself. While our paths diverged, our shared spirit of boldness endured. He took a chance then. I was now.

WHAT REALLY ICES THE CAKE, THOUGH, is how Aamish upends the entire central image of the essay—the "Indo-Nepali hope." His capacity to say "different Indo-Nepali" hope by the end reflects genuine growth. He hasn't abandoned his pursuit of greatness; he's merely adjusted the target. He hasn't abandoned his father's legacy; he's updating it to fit his own context. Life is now on his terms. The sprinkles on the cake are his brief descriptions of the Indian and American education systems and democratic histories, underlining the liberal-arts curiosity we mentioned before. This is a kid who's aware of his context. How many of his peers are so observant?

Authenticity

DO YOU LIKE HEROES WHO SIMPLY follow the path they're given and offer no glimpse into their personal thoughts or feelings (i.e. something literary scholars call "interiority")? Didn't think so. Luckily, Aamish keeps it plenty real throughout the essay. The sheer dread palpable in lines like "the only path there was" captures the weight of the "expectation" he mentions toward the beginning. Living in the shadow of his father has placed him into a box, and he desperately wishes to break free.

All this could easily veer into "woe is me" territory, but it manages to appear relatable (and likable) by resorting to one of our favorite devices: humor! When you read the whole bit on "pop-ups in my brain," you're inclined to give the kid a break. Brief as the moment is, it—along with the parenthetical "(spoiler alert: not great)"—provides just enough charm to confirm that this is no hyperserious, self-important candidate. He's capable of laughing at himself and even invites you to join along. Grandiosity becomes a concern only when you lack the ability to pop the balloon of your ego. Aamish's levity keeps him grounded amid what could otherwise be dismissed as whining. Who hasn't felt the crushing burden of filling someone else's shoes? The best heroes have weaknesses. The very best are courageous enough to discuss them.

Craft

IF THIS IS A SORT OF parallel origin story, and the two main characters are superheroes, then Aamish's narrative operates at several levels. That's always a plus, particularly when you're dealing with themes that are otherwise quite straightforward (like feeling the desire to become one's own man). One could say that Akhlak is the original superhero, the one who broke new ground, and that Aamish is the protégée destined to assume the mantle. Aamish could try to be a mere carbon copy of his father, but he has different ideas. Therefore, Akhlak serves not just as an invisible protagonist but also as the primary antagonist, in the purest sense. See, an "antagonist" is simply a character whose goals and values oppose those of the protagonist; by the end, the protagonist must challenge those opposing views and achieve a resolution resonating with their own value system. Batman and Joker. Superman and Lex Luthor. Professor X and Magneto. Akhlak isn't portrayed as a villain, of course, but he does provide tension for his son. Hence, we begin not with Aamish's story, but, like all great superhero stories (see *The Dark Knight's* famous opening scene), with the antagonist's story. The stark line, marking a specific date—"1998. A lone figure in a crowded train compartment"—functions as a framing device that circles back by the end. At first, we don't know who this person is, so we're curious. Just the fact that it's written in third-person perspective (instead of the usual first-person) builds intrigue. It solidifies Akhlak as a larger-than-life figure for Aamish. What does that say about our primary speaker? Why are we talking so much about the "antagonist"? Well, providing that context, that ghost of a presence—looming over everything Aamish does—gives him a problem to solve, an obstacle to overcome. Once he finally makes peace with it, Aamish can integrate the parts of his "enemy" that resonate with him. This is the maturity that so many superheroes gain when they defeat their own antagonistic force. Usually, the enemy isn't external but internal. As with Batman perennially being asked whether he should violate his #1 rule against killing, Aamish must complete the hero's journey by deciding what kind of a hero he's willing to be. The classic origin story genre was the perfect vehicle to capture that experience.

EXERCISE

Identify one personal hero or mentor figure in your life (real or fictional). How have you tried to live up to their example? How have you tried to forge your own separate path? Can your adoration and critique of this individual be reconciled?

From Chaos to Coherence: A Journey Through Numbers and Neurology

NIRBHIKA RAMANI

Delhi-NCR

Brown University

THERAPY. ONE TYPICALLY IMAGINES AN ANTIQUE room with leather sofas and a wise, soothing figure making mysterious notes on someone having a midlife crisis. So when I confess that I ended up in a therapist's office at the age of six, it invariably raises eyebrows.

Between role-playing to "discover my inner monsters," painting my feelings, and using my limited vocabulary to express my infuriation, my therapist and I embarked on a journey to discover why my temper tantrums and angsty fist-clenching got too much for my parents to handle.

The villains in my role-plays were adults who refused to explain their actions, and it became clear to my therapist that my behavior was not rooted in any traumatic event.

Instead, her descriptions (from notes I obtained from her ten years later) of my "resistance to meaningless instructions," "disagreements with norms taken for granted," and "an obsessive eye for detail" revealed that they were because of an all-consuming need to answer one fundamental question—why do people do what they do?

Naturally, nearly every attempt to garner an adequate explanation from adults left me dissatisfied. I passed hours in my room, silently reflecting on their statements, searching for contradictions, which I often discovered. And then the confused frustration would erupt again with redoubled force, causing me to withdraw from the world.

My parents worried that this withdrawal would worsen when I graduated from kindergarten and entered first grade. So did I, until I was greeted in my first class by a warm and unusually calm woman, carrying bags full of plastic blocks and evenly cut origami paper. That was the day that I discovered *Jodo Gyaan* (build knowledge), a tactile approach to mathematics.

As she joined blocks to show us why 5 times 5 is 25 and used a number line of beads to show what a prime number is, for the first time, everything was precise, black and white, with no subjective gray areas. There was a method, a function to transform input into output. This was the beginning of something new—the realization that a system existed to bring a semblance of order to the chaos that surrounded me.

However, I quickly realized the disparity between the safe bubble of math classes and the exasperating external world. Classroom mathematics was unable to answer my endless questions about human behavior. The dissatisfaction continued, more consuming than ever.

In the following years, my hunger was repeatedly refueled. When I was 12, I completed a Johns Hopkins CTY course on Inductive and Deductive Reasoning, which for the first time provided me with formal frameworks to understand the apparent malarkey inundating my senses.

Insights from philosophy and neuroscience about the operation of the human mind provided a significant breakthrough—theories that allowed me to accurately predict the outcomes of human interactions. When these disciplines were combined with mathematics, they began to reveal what I was searching for from birth—the rhythm of the universe, the music of the spheres.

These insights also helped me realize that therapy was simply a symptom of a deeper quest for knowledge.

This quest required blending my curiosity with patience. Instead of demanding answers from a world seemingly without order, I learned to translate its chaos into coherence, approaching every trial with the knowledge that I could calmly distill truth from turmoil. This radically transformed the nature of my interactions, replacing frustration with fulfillment. Realms of fear and confusion gave way to problems I could solve, people I connected to, and places where I finally belonged.

I seek, very simply, objective Truth. A data-driven enlightenment, if you will. It is an indomitable impulse, one that I have harbored since meticulously constructing towers from scattered blocks in my crib. These blocks have now evolved into information, but the fundamental need to structure them into something functional and beautiful—that remains and always will.

Summary

NIRBHIKA JOINED ATHENA IN 9TH GRADE, and we were immediately impressed by this young lady's precociousness! She could hold her own in debates with students years her senior, demonstrating a rare combination of IQ and EQ. Her arguments were crafted with pristine logic, but she could also acknowledge their shortcomings when applied to real-world situations. As a result, she gravitated toward the budding discipline of behavioral economics, which combines the rigor of mathematics with nuance of neuroscience, all in her endeavor to explain the puzzling occurrences she witnessed. Now, Nirbhika's essay never explicitly mentions "Behavioral Economics" (after all, it's a CAE and not an SOP). By the end, however, the reader has no doubt about her capacity to triumph in this field and beyond.

Values

WHERE TO BEGIN? THIS PIECE SCORES full points for Intellectual Vitality, as it highlights the author's deep, driving desire to unravel the mysteries of the cosmos. This is her primary reason for undergoing therapy, for she despises "meaningless instructions" and "norms taken for granted." Nirbhika desperately seeks the logical underpinnings behind the seemingly wayward actions of adults, and the absence of that unifying thread is immensely frustrating, leading to seemingly childish outbursts. Observing a yearning so primal, so genuine, we can't help but identify with her and root for her as she scales this philosophical mountain: "Why do people do what they do?"

Moreover, this unyielding drive for knowledge resonates with the primary objective of virtually every institute of higher learning: the discovery, documentation, and dissemination of humanity's intellectual treasures—now and forever. (This is particularly true of Brown, so dedicated to free thinking that their famous curriculum has no required core courses!) Nirbhika will undoubtedly serve as a most capable guardian of that wisdom.

Perspective

WE LOVE THE MOMENT WHEN NIRBHIKA'S therapist discovers the root of her struggle, which is presented in such a comical manner that you can't help but utter a chuckle: "The villains in my role-plays were adults who refused to explain their actions." Through these episodes, we observe Nirbhika's dawning realization, as she spends hours reflecting on the statements and behaviors of her "sinister" antagonists. Clever girl. But then, she discovers the magic of mathematics, through the *Jodo Gyaan* methodology, which reveals that not all life is a jumble of disconnected events; there are laws that govern the interactions of particles and people. Furthermore, she possesses the mystical capacity to wrap her mind around these explanations.

In every sentence, Nirbhika also underscores her liberal arts mindset, an educational approach we discuss throughout this book. American universities especially love scholars who can distill lessons from one domain and apply them to another, or apply frameworks from multiple fields to understand a complex concept. By demonstrating a budding competence in mathematics, philosophy, and neuroscience, Nirbhika signals to universities that she will intellectually engage with peers and even professors in a manner that enriches the classroom and campus as a whole. AOs resonate with a line like, "These insights also helped me realize that therapy was simply a symptom of a deeper quest for knowledge." It brings the essay full circle, showing that the theme transcends the realm of mental health; it's about "objective

Truth." Not too many students her age could make such an intriguing connection.

Authenticity

"THERAPY." A SINGLE-WORD OPENING SENTENCE. BANG. Talk about vulnerability. Even today, mental health remains a relatively taboo topic in India. Many aunties and uncles would see Nirbhika's line as airing dirty laundry. But again, it's the very brazenness of the introduction that captures the reader's attention. Especially when she announces at the paragraph's end that she's been sitting in these sessions since the age of six. The reader's response to such a confession is undoubtedly, "Who does that? Why is she undergoing treatment at such a tender age?"

With this expression of courage, Nirbhika draws us into her story from the very beginning. It leaves an impression that few readers can forget. How often do you see young authors willing to present themselves in a negative light? The image of how "my temper tantrums and angsty fist-clenching got too much for my parents to handle" is refreshingly candid. It feels like a young scientist recording her observations about a subject—which just so happens to be herself. This unflinching lack of bias, this utter lack of temptation to soften the edges of her self-portrait, earns our respect. We want to meet someone who's secure enough to confront her own flaws.

Craft

THERE'S BOTH TENSION AND HUMOR IN the first portion. The tension comes from a young girl who's clearly struggling. With what? We're eager to find out. However, the contrasting images of innocence and anger are also comical, especially given Nirbhika's tone. We love the range of the author's literary prowess, including sentences doused in delightful diction ("formal frameworks to understand the apparent malarkey inundating my senses") and phrases approaching pure poetry ("the rhythm of the universe, the music of the spheres"). This verbal virtuosity adds a fitting flourish to the mix, a charming contrast to the dense subject matter.

Finally, this piece presents a hard-hitting finale, the likes of which everyone must strive for. Nirbhika sums it all up so elegantly and powerfully, showcasing how her "indomitable impulse" has evolved over the years, from the blocks in her crib to intricate theories that require a similar process to build. The last line is dripping with both mind and heart, revealing that her passion for constructing "something functional and beautiful" will always remain, an indelible ingredient of her DNA. Precisely the DNA an elite institution wishes to introduce into its ranks.

EXERCISE

Discuss with your parents what you were like as a toddler or before the age of seven. Can you identify any characteristics that remain with you to this day? Are there any notable differences? What life experiences may account for those?

Larger Than Life: A Journey from Global Systems to Human Stories

ASHISH GOEL

Delhi-NCR

Brown University

I GRAVITATE TOWARD IDEAS, THEORIES, AND systems that can simply be described as "larger than life."

Films: state-of-the-art storytelling. A medium with stupendous reach, drawing eyes from across the globe—now embedded in the fabric of human culture.

Markets: growing infinitely, intricate webs woven within the world of economics. Countless exchanges and transactions, making me wonder whether money does, in fact, make the world go round.

Aviation: ferrying billions of travelers each year through airports, the focal nodes of international connectedness. I gape out of vast windows at fleets of magnificent jets, gargantuan feats of engineering, awed by their scale.

★ ★ ★

35,000 FEET

I live five miles from Indira Gandhi International Airport, the busiest in India. Often, as I drift asleep, I hear planes soar above, carrying my thoughts with them. My mind sweeps across open fields, crowded metropolises, and unforgiving oceans.

One might say I never had much trouble seeing the forest, undeterred by the trees.

Turbulence: fasten your seat belts!

Intent to meet those we were serving as part of the Healing Touch project, my friends and I journeyed to an elderly care home and shelter in Bhandwari, a village on Delhi's outskirts. While the voyage was short, it felt as though we had entered another sphere entirely.

A flurry of residents crowded the entrance, ready to greet the visitors they rarely received.

"May I borrow your phone? I need to hear my sister's voice," an anxious woman asked. As I dialed, she clutched my wrist. "Do you think she remembers me?" A volunteer promptly ushered her away, her protests drowned by the growing fervor.

Muzzy pictures of funeral rites hung on the mossy walls. Residents had come and gone, remembered only by portraits, adorned by withered garlands. Each individual bore a unique story laden with abandonment and destitution.

★ ★ ★

10,000 FEET

Here I was, studying resource allocation and demographic dividends, while these elders, the final vestiges of a bygone era, suffered. Adam Smith's Invisible Hand, a reassuring guide for policymakers, now seemed to slap me across the face.

Perhaps, no matter how robustly the web of economic systems was woven, its reliance on self-interest often allowed the marginalized to fall through the gaps.

My education and international exposure had made dealing in big-picture concepts convenient. Fulfilling my daily needs had never been a worry. Yet, while I sat in the big city, head amid the clouds, a woman in Bhandwari wondered where her next meal would come from.

★ ★ ★

1,000 FEET

"I wish we had more room. We've begun turning people away," a volunteer lamented.

Our guide accompanied us as we explored the home, interacting with the residents. A sense of urgency bubbled within; face after forlorn face tugged at my heartstrings.

"Now," she continued, "out of desperation, people leave their own elderly relatives tied to the front gates."

Utterly shaken, I awoke to the reality that macroeconomic trends comprised not only statistics and graphs, but also real human actors, each with a small, yet significant part on the world stage. I, too, had been cast in this larger human story. So, what role would I play?

I had to tap into my love for storytelling to exalt the unsung lives that made the world go round. My friends and I sprang into action, documenting their stories on social media while collecting funds and necessities from our community. We highlighted their faces, lest they be forgotten again. Through our efforts, we raised over 100,000 rupees for the construction of a second home, helping ensure that no one in need would have to be turned away.

Ideas can enact change at scale, but I must also ground myself in reality—find a synergy between abstract and concrete that closes the gaps.

A muted rumble as the plane touches down. Why just overlook a forest when you can take a trek through it, appreciating the beauty of each tree?

Summary

WELL, ASHISH GOEL HAD A PROBLEM. As an Indian male Delhite with an economics interest, he was a walking stereotype. Nothing interesting. Except—unlike so many of his peers from the same basket—he did have something that elite universities value: high-mindedness. What do we mean? While most Indian students reflect the more straightforward, goal-oriented ethos of the Indian education system (which contrasts greatly with that of the US), Ashish liked to *think*. He had genuine extracurriculars that he'd pursued in depth. These elements defied expectations. Even better, although his Tier- 1 city bred countless international applicants every year, Ashish specifically lived near the airport and had something intriguing to say about it. So, we had a brand to showcase: Delhi-based Indian male+liberal arts economics-meets-service-meets-film-

making interest. It was a Leadership/Service Profile that distinguished
itself through his uniquely expansive perspective. When it comes
to college application essays, that may just do the trick! The only
problem was that we needed the CAE to represent his pretentious
macro-view orientation in a winsome manner and not a negative one
(our best bet since demographics provided essentially no hooks).
Challenge accepted.

Values

AT HIS CORE, ASHISH IS AN intellectual. This is good, because elite
American universities cherish the ideal of intellectualism. They don't
call them the "ivory tower" for nothing! Heady discussions of liberal
arts topics like the role of film, markets, and aviation in society reflect
an uncommon capacity for independent thought. But instead of
speaking in vague generalities, Ashish keeps everything specific. He has
a theme, based on the idea of the macro. And it contrasts sharply with
that of community, which arises soon after the opening section. Were
he a mere thinker, he'd appear hollow, detached, cold. His devotion
to a cause greater than himself tethers him to the real world. There's
compassion, demonstrated through his interest in the residents' stories,
which he portrays through scenes of dialogue. This attention to detail
gives humanity to the individuals instead of painting everyone in broad
strokes. As a result, we feel his empathy when he describes how "face
after forlorn face tugged at my heartstrings." We see his altruistic desire
to help improve their lives through fundraising and filmmaking, which
reads genuine instead of falling into the Project Essay or Do-Gooder
Essay trap. Through the creative initiative he devises, Ashish presents
himself as a positive force we can believe in.

Perspective

A PHILOSOPHICAL ESSAY SUCH AS THIS one better offer some novel
thoughts. And thankfully, it delivers. Ashish's musings linger on the
idea of scale, ultimately uncovering that—and here's our favorite word
again—*nuance* is the key to resolving his problem. At several points,
he identifies additional layers in his conflict—the reliance of economic
systems on "self-interest" and the "marginalization" of disadvantaged
populations—ultimately reaching a conclusion that deeply satisfies.

Resisting the temptation to simply dismiss his previous tendencies entirely, Ashish must "find a synergy between abstract and concrete that closes the gaps." It's a truly mature development that most students his age have yet to make. Even adults often struggle with this. The Greeks had a central tenet, arguing for "Nothing in excess." The Romans understood it as temperantia, or "moderation." Christians took this "cardinal virtue" and framed it as one of their Seven Holy Virtues, believing that extremes—of anything—could be dangerous. You find similar views throughout world traditions, from Aristotle's Golden Mean to Buddhism's Middle Path. True wisdom is the ability to integrate opposites instead of rejecting them. Ashish proves precocious here, a modern-day yogi!

Authenticity

ALL THIS GREAT BRAININESS AND SERVICE would be for naught if Ashish couldn't present a compelling persona. His #1 danger in this essay was appearing frigid, the classic problem for all intellectuals. Fundamentally, the reader must be able to connect with the author. Every action must be accompanied by human warmth, even when the action is ostensibly positive. This is where we must address the question of the so-called "literate" writer. They're always pretentious. Now, because pretentiousness is a double-edged sword—elite universities love it—we can use a trick that applies far beyond college applications. If you view things the right way, every strength is a weakness, and every weakness is a strength. Ashish embraces his steely exterior by presenting it upfront and allowing it to crack, then eventually letting it crumble throughout the course of the narrative. It's a classic move to preempt any accusations of tone deafness. Great stories usually center on a protagonist who begins one way and ends up another. In other words, they undergo a growth journey.

And there need not be one lone Pivot that occurs at the end; here, we have multiple, reflecting the ongoing evolution of Ashish's thought process and emotional maturation. Look at how he gets honest with us in the middle of the plot:

> My education and international exposure had made dealing in big-picture concepts convenient. Fulfilling my daily needs had never been a worry. Yet, while I sat in the big city, head amid the clouds, a woman in Bhandwari wondered where her next meal would come from.

Does this sound like a kid with a savior complex (anymore)? Does he sound arrogant now? In a bit of wordplay on an age-old idiom, he's willing to admit that his ability to see the "forest for the trees" has been foolish, nothing to be proud of. The second half of the essay is a comeuppance—or perhaps a "comedownance"—bringing Ashish off his high horse to become more grounded, closer to earth. Most heroes are interesting because they experience character development, a fundamental change in personality that makes them a better person. Ashish's arc is upward, which contrasts wonderfully with his landing.

Craft

AS WE'VE SHOWN BEFORE, ONE OF the best ways to make an impression is to begin with a punchy opening line. "I gravitate toward ideas, theories, and systems that can simply be described as larger than life." Anyone who reads that is bound to consider the author grandiose and perhaps a bit conceited—but they'll want to know more. That's how hooks work—they hook your attention. You continue, and find Ashish establishing the evidence of his "larger than life" interests, which indeed appear more advanced than your average high schooler's.

You might assume the essay will continue along this track, but then it shifts abruptly. What we get is a structure that fits Ashish's perspective perfectly: an airline "descent" framing device for an author obsessed with airports! Each section features the pilot's message to the cabin (from declining altitude to warnings of turbulence), signifying a slow approach toward Ashish's enlightenment. By the end, he's fully on the tarmac, capable of seeing the "trees" he'd always ignored in the past. Interspersed throughout are distinct word choices that reflect real care and deliberate images. "Focal nodes," "gargantuan," "flurry of residents," "muzzy," and "withered garlands" all serve to capture Ashish's cinematic experience in detail, so we too can see it through his eyes. Would you have expected that from a standard Indian male Delhite with an economics interest?

EXERCISE

What are some big ideas that preoccupy your mind? Do others fail to share an appreciation for this interest or perspective? Do you take pride in your approach? Why or why not?

Dissolving Boundaries:
A Tale of Two Cultures
in One Soul

NEEL MALHOTRA

Mumbai

Yale University

NEEL - *BLUE* LIKE WATER

I often wonder what would have happened had I popped out on a plane. Would I be a citizen of some North Atlantic island? Ireland, perhaps?

I was going to be born in Rochester, New York. But my mother wanted a son as *desi* as they come. Thus began the much-recounted adventure of how she boarded Air India to New Delhi, just a few weeks before I was due. And just like that, my cultural roots were rerouted.

But why would my mother come all the way back here to give birth to me? What was so fascinating about this land of sweltering sun and teeming towns? What was the nature of this "Indianness" that she so devotedly strove to inculcate in me?

My mother and extended family, exhausted from a preteen's barrage of questions on the matter, referred me to books on Indian history and mythology. I chronicled the rise and fall of dynasties, exotic traders, would-be colonizers, the coexistence of contrasting religions and cultures functioning together as the most complex democracy in the world.

But the more I read, the more confused I grew. Amid the multifaceted patchwork of geography and demography, what was the common element that unified "India?" And how did "India" connect to Neel?

Perplexed, I decided to set aside the history books and consult a man with direct knowledge of history. My grandfather was a freedom fighter in the Indian Independence Movement; if anyone in my family understood the soul of the nation, it was someone who had fought for its creation.

My grandfather simply listened to my dilemma and smiled: "Neel, water dissolves all materials, and they become part of the water. This is India. It has absorbed and integrated waves of invaders and immigrants—Persian, Mughal, British, American—everyone bringing something new and valuable: from ornate architectural structures, to elaborate administrative systems, to sophisticated high-tech firms." And this is the India that has stood the test of time, renewing itself through centuries into a more perfect whole.

And, this is the Indian in me.

Like India, I too engage with diversity, and after each interaction, I imbibe the rich elements of others. Whether it is discussing the characteristics of Ahura Mazda with my Zoroastrian peers, or conversing with Mumbaikars on trains that crisscross the city, hearing stories of stalwart migrants who have traversed half the country to seek work, I am always eager to come into contact with difference, share experiences, and emerge stronger, renewed by everything from philosophical discourses to inspiring tales.

But the story does not end here.

On one occasion, fiddling with an American quarter, I discovered the Latin words *E Pluribus Unum* (Out of many, one). Everything that applied to India applied to America, which is also a product of waves of immigrants, all bringing unique value to its shores, adding to the robust pluralism of the land. So, ironically, what makes me Indian also makes me American!

This is what my mother wanted to preserve in her little boy.

"Neel, you were named blue because we wanted you to be like water—molding, shaping, adapting, evolving, to encompass everything and transcend all boundaries."

The same way that Columbus had set off to discover India, and found America instead, I had too. But more importantly, I had found myself. In scrutinizing the dilemma of my existence, I had discovered that there was none. The idea of India is the idea of America and the idea of Neel—blue like water that absorbs the best and dissolves differences.

My acceptance and appreciation of multi-dimensional perspectives, my belief that every point of view brings knowledge and wisdom, as well as my optimism that every diverse entity has something to teach me—this is the core that constructs me, defines me, enlightens me.

Summary

HERE AGAIN, WE WITNESS AN ALL-TOO-FAMILIAR struggle: how do we add that special sauce, that "masala factor" to a smart lad's profile, so he doesn't come off as your everyday Indian nerd? We tirelessly sought some hook to play with, and after pursuing countless dead ends, finally settled on the most personal of topics for a personal essay: one's own name. Moreover, Neel also dug deep to provide a unique take on the standard immigrant story, uncovering powerful insights into the essence of different cultures and their underlying similarities. What we're left with is a piece that showcases the applicant's unique capacity for reflection, introspection, even meditation—a trait in short supply among hard-nosed STEM-mies.

Values

WE WERE STRUCK BY THE PHRASE "a preteen's barrage of questions." For a twelve-year-old to pursue answers so relentlessly (when there's no test at the end of the week) is a mark of true intellectual vitality, an intrinsic desire to know more. Curiosity is essential to expanding humanity's horizons, regardless of the field, so this little tidbit is an undeniable signal to admissions officers that the student will fit appropriately, perhaps even ideally, within the campus community.

Neel also highlights, on multiple occasions, his cultural rootedness. He isn't dismissive of his tradition, but instead appreciates that the past shapes the present, and that his past shapes the man he's becoming. The expansiveness of his reading list ("books on Indian history and mythology") is another intellectual flex, revealing to us that this scholar can crunch complex information from multiple interdisciplinary sources in his endeavor to uncover insights about himself and his surroundings.

Finally, Neel's other core values emerge toward the end of the piece. He muses on how water takes the shape of its container, and flows uninhibited across any surface, dissolving barriers and unifying disparate elements. The metaphor describes Neel, too: he transcends limiting labels, drawing strength from the diversity of people and experiences in his life. This cosmopolitan mindset is a hallmark of all progressive institutions, especially global universities like Yale. Therefore, they're always keen to see young people who embrace a similarly expansive view of the world and its inhabitants.

Perspective

THE MAJOR INSIGHT IN THIS ESSAY comes not from Neel, but from his dear grandfather (you owe him one, young man!). However, we accept this "Grandpa Ex Machina" moment since Neel clearly did his own homework and attempted to unwrap the thorny conundrum before approaching others. We see the effort he invests in reading diverse texts, and are thus forgiving when he consults his lifeline. And what a lifeline it is! Grandpa so eloquently captures the kernel of India, the philosophical core that has defined the place for millennia. On top of that, he helps Neel understand how his own name connects to the idea of India, shedding light on the opening mystery of his mother's decision. The way the country has engaged with foreign waves over the centuries is also how Neel himself interacts with everyone in his life— how can one absorb something novel, incorporate it into one's identity, and come back with renewed vigor?

But Neel doesn't let Grandpa do all the thinking for him! We also love the kicker, the discovery of America's motto on the back of a quarter. This exhibits one of our favorite concepts: higher-order thinking skills, or "HOTS." Neel connects what his grandfather recounted with a Latin phrase, and with that connection surmises that there's no contradiction between his Indian and American selves; they both embrace pluralism by learning from diverse individuals. To offer something obvious, like ending the story at his newfound appreciation for India's diversity, would be an exercise in *lower-order thinking skills*. Thankfully, he has LOTS more profundity to share. As Neel powerfully sums it up: "In scrutinizing the dilemma of my existence, I had discovered that there was none."

Authenticity

EVEN IN THIS FAIRLY INTELLECTUAL ESSAY, we can't overlook the importance of vulnerability. As intelligent as Neel is, he isn't afraid to admit his confusion and ask the most (seemingly) basic of questions aloud: "And how did 'India' connect to Neel?" Remember, admissions officers don't expect 17-year-olds to have all the answers (and projecting such authority would be counterproductive, to say the least). Surprisingly, they're more impressed with the students who are hard at work progressively diminishing their own ignorance. That's Neel. He takes us on an adventure, a journey of self-discovery in which he grows wiser by the paragraph. And if a pupil can demonstrate this level of growth over the span of an essay, imagine the heights to which he'll scale over four years at Yale.

Craft

THE ESSAY'S HOOK IS EXQUISITE: "I often wonder what would have happened had I popped out on a plane." As the reader, you're already wondering what's going on. Why is this young man even contemplating his birth mid-air? What extraordinary circumstances could've led to such a possibility?

Then, in the next paragraph, this mystery is solved—Mom wanted it—but that only opens another can of worms. Why was Neel's mother so insistent on his being born in India? This question sets the stage for the entire piece. And that story is told so marvelously, replete with vibrant language that relieves any tedium the reader may be experiencing. From the alliteration of the "sweltering sun and teeming towns" to the rerouting wordplay to the peppering of Indianisms like *desi*, we're taken along on a wondrous ride. In the process, we come to understand Neel Malhotra as much as anyone can in 650 words.

EXERCISE

What does your name mean? Is it accurate? Have you grown toward your name in time? Or perhaps away? Is there a way you can reinterpret your name to fully own it?

QUEST FOR THE THEORY OF EVERYTHING: CHASING THE FUNDAMENTAL LAWS OF REALITY

HARSH DUTTA

Delhi-NCR

Harvard University

FROM CHILDHOOD, I HAVE HAD AN insatiable yearning to understand "everything." I needed to comprehend the underlying principles that explained the diverse phenomena I witnessed in nature, from the taste of ice cream to the dissolution of stars.

The questioning was incessant. In science class, when I learned one theory, I would search my mental database for related theories. Was there a conflict between two theories? Was one or both of them partly or fully wrong? Was there a more general theory that reconciled the two? All these questions were subsets of my seemingly ridiculous meta-question: How does it all work? Each question I answered led to more alluring general questions. It was, as a teacher joked, "an almost neurotic obsession."

However, at some point, this yearning for a "Theory of Everything" confused me. Was this impetus conducive to becoming a scientist? Was I too "distracted" to develop a specialization? Wasn't a scientist supposed to understand a particular domain—biologists, organisms; astrophysicists, stars and planets? Could my quest to identify the fundamental laws governing all reality be considered science? Or was science about problem-solving and building machines to enhance human life? Or finally, was science merely accidental discovery—the way Alexander Fleming found penicillin? What was science, after all?

I found my answer halfway across the world, during an internship at CERN in the summer after tenth grade. CERN brought scientists from over 100 countries together in the quest to understand our universe. I saw people driven by curiosity and a deep desire to discover new knowledge about our universe. The environment instantly resonated with my state of mind. From these laboratories came revolutionary theories of supersymmetry, antimatter, and digital physics—concepts that help us unravel the fabric of reality. From my interactions, I realized that every one of these scientists was in pursuit of the "Theory of Everything." I was overjoyed to meet John Ellis, the man behind this term, as he explained to me the significance behind the equations on his t-shirt: a concise version of the *Lagrangian* that encompasses everything we know about the universe, from supernovae to the blossoming of roses.

However, reflecting on CERN and other experiences, I began to realize that there may be limits to our ability to grasp the Whole. Heisenberg's Uncertainty Principle, Godel's Incompleteness Theorem, and the P-NP problem all suggest that some mysteries may never be solved. This was corroborated by Greek philosophers such as Parmenides, who argued that a mind trapped in three dimensions cannot comprehend the Whole of which it is but a part.

Nevertheless, despite appreciating these limits, the CERN scientists continued their blissful pursuit of knowledge. They helped me understand that the "Theory of Everything" might be an unattainable asymptote; however, they continued seeking answers sincerely and relentlessly. They were happy running on a treadmill that never stops and that never led to any particular final destination. A theory of everything might never be attained, but its pursuit is noble. Science is nothing but this pursuit. This was my epiphany. Physicists are modern explorers, sailing vast oceans of ignorance in search of new lands and insights. Galileo, Newton, Einstein, Tesla, Higgs—all were motivated day and night to identify general theories that explained a wide range of phenomena.

I had a personal encounter with the "Theory of Everything" during the All-India Linguistics Olympiad Training Camp, where I applied Benford's Law—a statistical concept that explains the relative sizes of craters, lakes and cities—to decipher a strange language based on the distribution of words. I never before thought a single theory could apply to both geographic landforms and a human construct like language.

And this is what my life is about. I want to discover new truths that the universe divulges, and use those general truths to explain a variety of phenomena and solve problems that confront our species.

Summary

WE AT ATHENA ARE ALWAYS THRILLED by students who wish to pursue the pure sciences. Academics at heart, we love scholars motivated by the unadulterated pursuit of knowledge, for whom its various applications are but a side note. Harsh was one such pupil, a physics lover dedicated to understanding how the cosmos operates in seemingly mysterious ways. This impulse formed the cornerstone of his identity, and so, we could think of no better subject for Harsh's Common Application Essay. What emerged was the portrait of a truly sublime thinker, one who'll no doubt contribute to scientific advancement over a long and illustrious career—with a healthy touch of humor, of course!

Values

HARSH BEGINS BY GOING STRAIGHT TO his core, declaring in no uncertain terms his insatiable yearning to understand "everything." He elaborates with a poetic statement highlighting the sheer breadth of his thought, spanning both the micro and the macro: "I needed to comprehend the underlying principles that explained the diverse phenomena I witnessed in nature, from the taste of ice cream to the dissolution of stars." Therefore, even after reading just one paragraph, we feel that we know Harsh; we resonate with his noble aspiration to uncover the principles that govern the material universe. This value of seeking profound knowledge, the general laws that underlie existence, is the lifeblood and driving force of the piece. It's what makes Harsh a scholar who lives the quintessential—our favorite term again—"life of the mind." You can just picture him graduating from Harvard summa cum laude, heading off to a similar institution for his doctorate, then becoming the next Gödel, Heisenberg, or Hawking. And the Nobel Prize goes to...

Perspective

HARSH'S WRITING IS PEPPERED WITH EXAMPLES of how systematically he thinks, which is almost artful in its simplicity. He takes us through a whole series of questions in the second paragraph, which reveals to the reader how he processes information. It is precisely the manner in which physicists and philosophers devise structures of thought, identifying first principles and painstakingly building upon those foundations to erect intellectual cathedrals. This isn't easy; it requires immense patience and energy, but Harsh is more than happy to undertake this challenge if it'll bring him closer to his Ultimate Aim.

More insights arise when Harsh first enters CERN, which can only be described as a butterfly in a nursery, eager to consume as much delectable nectar as possible. At this legendary institution, Harsh realizes that while his seemingly outlandish commitment to theoretical physics isn't mainstream, there are close-knit communities around the world that can think of nothing better than to contemplate the nature of the universe. Now, for the first time, he can open his mind and heart and be unapologetically himself. However, this isn't his concern. Harsh doesn't want acceptance; he simply wants collaborators who can help him achieve his Ultimate Aim. And in Switzerland, he finds a high concentration of them, many of whom provide him with precisely the conceptual breakthroughs he needs to continue his journey. After the internship, Harsh understands that academic physics is exploration— there's never a guarantee something grand will be unveiled. However, he owes it to himself, the physics community, and the world at large (not to mention his idols of the past) to give it his all, to even run perpetually on the treadmill to nowhere for a mere possibility of discovering something transformative. His beloved Theory of Everything may be an "unattainable asymptote," but that doesn't stop him from pressing on toward the horizon. And while he hasn't achieved his Ultimate Aim just yet, he does make a breakthrough by applying Benford's law in two seemingly unrelated domains: geographic formations and linguistic patterns. A first of many steps in the right direction.

Authenticity

THE MORE YOU KNOW, THE LESS you're afraid of admitting your own ignorance. The ancient Greeks praised this virtue of courageous humility, proclaiming "Surety brings ruin" as one of their core tenets. And let's not forget the legendary philosopher Socrates—namesake of the Socratic method that shapes the ethos of Western pedagogy—who famously uttered, "I know that I know nothing." Moreover, Richard Feynman, one of the most respected physicists of the 20th century, often commented on how little he understood the machinations of the atom. While Harsh is not (yet) at Feynman's level, his willingness to reveal the limits of his (current) abilities is a bold signaling technique.

Only an exceptional mind would so unabashedly spotlight its own shortcomings, as we see in the third paragraph, where Harsh expresses his confusion regarding the very nature of science. In confessing doubts about whether he's actually cut out for an academic life, he invites us to experience the same emotions he faces. "Confused" and "distracted" may be negative states, but they're honest. Everyone feels them from time to time. And it's essential that Harsh opens this window into his soul, since so many students of his demographic assume that they have to keep their souls shuttered. The prevailing male STEM stereotype is the impassive "intellectual" (like Sheldon from The Big Bang Theory), devoid of the capacity to feel. Such individuals seem to lack interior lives—ups, downs, frustration, elation—which makes them difficult to care about. Your goal throughout the application journey? Make the admissions officers *care* about you. They have to feel invested. Now, we don't know about you, but we certainly want to see the next stage of Harsh's holistic growth.

Craft

DENSE MATERIAL ALWAYS BENEFITS FROM A bit of comic relief. We see this in Shakespeare's tragedies: as the fateful inter-family conflict rages, Mercutio mocks his cousin Romeo, declaring him a foolishly hopeless romantic. Harsh, on the other hand, punctuates his discussion on the Theory of Everything with a humorous statement from a teacher, who at once praises and politely mocks the young man's "almost neurotic obsession."

And to top it off, Harsh quotes not only physics, but also math, computer science—even philosophy and geography! A truly liberal artist, soon to become a Gentleman of Harvard.

EXERCISE

Take your favorite academic discipline. What are the foundational principles upon which it's built? Can you generate a set of maxims that applies in all cases? If not, get as close as possible, and identify the limits of your personal "Theory of Everything."

INK FROM TEARS: CRAFTING POETRY FROM PAIN

CHAHAT MAHESHWARI

Delhi-NCR

University of Pennsylvania

"These poems are regarding human life as a whole and the various phases of life."

~Ripples of the Mind.

WHEN I WROTE *RIPPLES OF THE MIND* in tenth grade, I knew I was writing out of pervasive melancholia. Tears, fears, and drama are the ingredients that cook the savory teenage years. Heartbreaks are considered "common," even "normal."

However, severing ties with my best friend didn't feel "normal."

I still remember how caring she was when a close relative passed away. Little did I know that I would soon receive a rude awakening. While she sent me a text "How are you, BFF?," she simultaneously messaged an acquaintance, "Chahat's the worst, unfriend her." It was hurtful to learn that one of my closest friends now despised me. I tried confronting her, only to be dismissed and eventually shunned.

The screenshot spread like wildfire. As I walked into class the next day, sweat trickled down my face. I knew that all eyes were on me, and soon, the number of people in a room became directly proportional to my loneliness.

My tears became the ink with which I penned down my poems.

★ ★ ★

Lights on,
And I'm covered with a threatening mask. ~Pg 70

A voice in my head taunted: "You aren't worth it." I found myself in an endless spiral of self-doubt—was I the reason? Every time I looked at my reflection, the self-loathing grew stronger. Confined and unable to share my pain with anyone, I found solace in poetry.

I wrote non-stop. Poetry was the one place where I was honest about my feelings, the one place where I confronted myself. I felt the pages talk back to me, and the writer needed to listen. But was this conversation enough to illuminate the recesses of my mind, those too painful to behold?

Little did I know, hidden in my poems were answers I was unaware I'd written.

★ ★ ★

All she had to do,
Was inform her crew. ~Pg 51

I shared fragments of my writing with my mother. As I spoke each verse, revealing the weight of grief it carried, a subtle peace emerged. The air of isolation started to dissipate. While writing felt like a safe space, sharing helped me face my fears. I started slowly, posting one poem at a time on my private Instagram. "A desperate call for attention," was one comment. "You'll become a laughingstock," was another.

But I kept going, kept embracing the pain. I realized that the intensity of will it took to break the barriers was double the work necessary to create them. For the longest time, it was harrowing to be honest about my feelings beyond the four walls of my room.

Until I published *Ripples of the Mind*.

Recounting some of my darkest personal struggles in front of a large audience was strangely empowering. I answered people's questions earnestly; later, several teenagers came up to me to talk about how they related to my book. I did receive many unpleasant comments on the heartbreak section of my poems since I was "only a teenager." However, I shrugged off the hate, since what mattered was that I had finally put my story out there.

Writing, sharing, and performing poems became a flashlight in the metaphoric cave I was trapped in.

As I flipped through the pages of the last chapter, something was revealed: an appreciation for not retreating from fear when our heartstrings stretch, or even snap. Although heartbreaks can be arduous, we may rediscover ourselves in the process and find attachment to greater loves—for me, it was my work as a poetess and the people with whom my verses resonated.

Now, when I stand in front of the mirror, I no longer shy away from my reflection, no matter the ripples that may come my way.

> *Your tears never stop*
> *But neither do you*
> *You never give up. ~Pg 76*

Summary

THE AMERICAN HIGHER EDUCATION SYSTEM HAS its origins in ancient Greece, where the educational ideal was synthetic: uniting the sciences and the arts (as well as athletics, hence the birth of the Olympics). In recent years, this ideal has been distilled into the acronym STEAM, which adds "Art" to the customary "Science, Technology, Engineering, and Mathematics." The author of the following piece embodies this; while she's an Indian female computer science aspirant, you'd never know it from her CAE. Smartly, she uses the opportunity to discuss (and display!) her poetic prowess, clarifying to universities that she's far from a one-trick pony. The reason this ability is so critical even for a science student is that countless innovations arise from cross-disciplinary engagement. Chahat's skills in both computer science and the literary arts is an indication of the multifaceted scholar she'll be, and the many insights she'll bring to her college community. But there's more! Through her story, Chahat also showcases the profound emotional growth she undergoes as a result of her teenage tribulations. What results is a beautiful coming-of-age story ripe with profundity and intensity.

Values

ANTIFRAGILITY IS ONE QUALITY AMERICAN UNIVERSITIES particularly prize. It's highly correlated with success across a range of activities. Antifragility, in our minds, is a more advanced form of grit: one not only presses on through difficult terrain, but also embraces the ordeal and grows stronger with every step. Colleges are so appreciative of this trait that one of the Common Application Essay prompts asks students the following:

> The lessons we take from obstacles we encounter can be fundamental to later success. Recount a time when you faced a challenge, setback, or failure. How did it affect you, and what did you learn from the experience?

In this spirit, Chahat "kept embracing the pain" when the going got tough, understanding that she was being remade into something greater. She couples this idea with an extremely poignant point, one communicated with such panache that images and sounds inevitably emerge in the reader's mind: ."..not retreating from fear when our heartstrings stretch, or even snap."

This young lady is beginning to witness some of the less flattering elements of life. However, instead of growing bitter, she sublimates her struggle into a talent, as many great artists do: "For the longest time, it was harrowing to be honest about my feelings beyond the four walls of my room. Until I published *Ripples of the Mind*." She cherishes the value of revealing even what makes her uncomfortable. Or rather, especially what makes her comfortable. As she matures, she learns to ignore the haters and present her story without holding back.

Perspective

THE VOICE INSIDE ONE'S HEAD ISN'T always true. This is a profound insight for a teenager; alas, most adults still struggle to grasp it. Chahat's description of her initial attempts at writing are nothing short of magical. The pages mystically respond to her suffering. It's as though her penned thoughts have a life of their own: "hidden in my poems were answers I was unaware I'd written." But it isn't just writing; the act of sharing is cathartic, allowing her to transform fear into wisdom. When she publishes her book, she takes this thought even further, serving as a channel for others with similar experiences. "Writing, sharing, and performing poems became a flashlight in the metaphoric cave I was trapped in." A computer science scholar who arrives at metaphors like that? She's the real deal indeed.

Authenticity

FALLING OUT WITH A BEST FRIEND is a quintessential adolescent experience. However, the manner in which Chahat recounts her story is wrenching, from the unexpected duplicity to the rampant cyber-bullying that rendered every moment in class unbearable. She takes us through her downward spiral, introducing the self-doubt and eventually the self-loathing. Even when she finally musters the courage to share her work, she must face comments like "A desperate call for attention" and "You'll become a laughingstock." Yet, she leans into the discomfort, knowing full well that on the other side, transformation awaits. The only way to reach the light is by passing through the tunnel.

Craft

CHAHAT BEGINS THE PIECE BY QUOTING herself. A daring move, but one she gets away with given the sheer poetry of the opening paragraphs. It's not every day you see a teenager employ phrases like "pervasive melancholia" with such flair. Moreover, we were captivated by many of her following lines, which demonstrate a budding capacity to mold words into sharp images and internal rhymes: "Tears, fears, and drama are the ingredients that cook the savory teenage years." She also includes statements steeped in ironic wit, such as "the number of people in a room became directly proportional to my loneliness."

And finally, the powerful inflection point, in which she sublimates all the heartache into art: "My tears became the ink with which I penned down my poems." The resulting journey captures the fragmented nature of Chahat's experience, ultimately making her whole. Her choice to have each section feature an excerpt from her book feels absolutely integral to the story she wishes to tell. It confirms to us that this is a genuine young poetess with immense potential in many domains. She's bound to make more than just ripples in her future community.

EXERCISE

Name an art, sport, or other activity you perform on a regular basis. How can you infuse that activity with your character, personality, background, or anything else unique?

Beyond the Flag: Realizing the Impact of Inclusive Politics

ANMOL JAIN

Delhi-NCR

University of Pennsylvania

"YOU'VE GROWN SO MUCH! IT FEELS like we went to the Jan Lokpal protest just yesterday. I even have a picture from that day!"

Vishal uncle was visiting us after a decade. I sat with my family, listening to him narrate tales from his adventures abroad.

"Enough about me. Anmol, tell me about yourself."

"Um…I'm in 11th grade. My subjects are…"

"None of that boring stuff!"

"I…don't know," I stammered.

There was one dreaded request that marked the beginning of all interactions with unfamiliar people: *Tell me about yourself.* While I always had a standard response prepared, it hadn't impressed Vishal uncle.

I lay awake that night looking at the picture he was referring to. Seven-year-old me was waving the Indian flag. I had been taken to a peaceful protest for increased governmental transparency. Inspired by the enthusiastic crowd, I wanted to learn about the reasons behind the event.

Badgering my teachers and family with questions about governmental systems and policy creation, I was hungry to satiate my curiosity.

It dawned on me that the protest had significantly impacted the course of my life. Curious to uncover other such moments, I dug out old family photo albums. Leafing through the pages, I came across 13-year-old me standing next to Khalid, a cab driver I met during a trip to Russia. His gruff voice echoed in my mind:

"We had to run away from Chechnya."

"But you have a right to self-determination!"

"Boy, things don't work like that. This is the real world."

Until then, I had assumed that even if people were unhappy, they always had ways to voice their concerns. After all, wasn't democracy for, of, and by the people? Learning that almost 1.5 million Chechens lived in a reality they couldn't escape sobered my naivete. Bidding Khalid an uncomfortable goodbye, I wondered if any Indians shared his predicament.

As a foreigner, I couldn't do much for the Chechen people, but perhaps things could be different at home. My research strategy evolved as I began to look for cracks in India's political and economic system and sought out communities that had fallen through them.

"Taking up Indian citizenship will dilute our cause. We are Tibetan, not Indian or Chinese."

My phone's photo gallery yielded a picture of an old monk in a saffron robe. Investigating further led me to Majnu ka Tila, Delhi's Tibetan colony, and to Lobsang, a refugee residing in the area. Unable to vote in elections due to its non-citizen status, the community faced marginalization at every turn. Armed with a plan, I helped community members sign up for Permanent Account Number (PAN) cards, which would allow them to avail relief schemes offered by the government while retaining their Tibetan identity.

From observer to organizer, I had come a long way since my first encounter with politics. Revisiting my journey lent me a renewed sense of self.

Every community I have interacted with has faced its own unique challenges. Some communities get their voices heard, while some are left helpless. As our lives become more insulated, we tend to disregard the narratives of those who don't share our reality.

Just as the Indian independence movement evolved from a mere anti-colonial campaign to one that included various visions for an economically developed, secular, democratic republic, our shared visions for India today will help herald our nation into the new global era.

I want to rekindle our faded historical memory and strengthen collective resolve by inspiring individuals to participate in active citizenship. Through engagement and action, many lives can be revolutionized.

Like the political landscape, my identity, too, is constantly transforming. Idealistic as it may sound, I am determined in my resolve to include every narrative in political discourse. I am confident that united, we can catalyze consequential change.

This I'll say to the next person who asks me to tell them about myself.

Summary

ANMOL JAIN. A STRAIGHTFORWARD, SOFT-SPOKEN CHAP whose unassuming exterior belied a passionate spirit underneath. At first glance, you might've written him off as yet another Indian male Delhiite (take a number!), but then you also might've overlooked the elements that made him interesting. Instead of following a typical STEM or economics/business track, Anmol was pursuing the humanities. His distinct social science–social activism–social entrepreneurship angle gave him a Leadership/Service Profile that united diverse issues and lines of thinking. In other words, it was uncommon, and uncommon is good. While he didn't entirely belong to the community he cared about, Anmol had demonstrated real concern through action. He put his money where his mouth was. Thus, the Project/Activity Essay trope made perfect sense to showcase this quality. We just needed to elevate it beyond the stock Do-Gooder clichés by keeping it personal. (After all, the CAE is called a "personal essay" for a reason!) The refreshing voice we discovered along the way completely upended stereotypes, as all genuine voices do.

Values

DON'T YOU JUST WANT TO ROOT for this kid? From the very beginning, it's clear that he's a listener. Instead of being a showboat, braggart, or egotist seeking all the attention, he simply wishes to hear his uncle recount stories. Talk about self-effacing. Anmol's entire conflict is centered on how uncomfortable he feels making things about himself.

What this tension reveals is a virtuous human being who truly loves others. Driven by undeniable Intellectual Vitality, he's hungry "to satiate [his] curiosity" regarding "governmental systems and policy creation."

But it isn't just an abstract, theoretical interest. Whether it's with political concepts or social interactions, Anmol wishes to absorb knowledge so he can actually act on it. Going "from observer to organizer," he assumes the identity of an advocate and volunteer. The journey takes him to a group of marginalized residents he never even knew existed. Compassion of this order—the ability to care about others even when their fate doesn't directly affect you—reflects a special kind of altruism. For Anmol is driven by the same high-minded ideals of democracy and inclusivity that define progressive institutions like Penn, itself seated in the very city where the Declaration of Independence was signed. "I am confident that united," he writes, "we can catalyze consequential change." This young champion of "active citizenship" is a leader. Even his preachings (for several paragraphs!) at the end demonstrate a humble yet fiery ambition and tenacity. "Idealistic as it may sound, I am determined in my resolve to include every narrative in political discourse." We have no doubt that he'll inspire many others to the call of duty.

Perspective

WAIT, ARE HIGH-SCHOOLERS EXPECTED TO POSSESS this much profundity? Because certainly, Anmol presents surprising sophistication in how he recognizes macro social ills. Indeed, that word sophistication defines the entire discussion. Anmol addresses weighty issues that transcend his specific local context, adopting instead a nuanced, global perspective. He takes a seemingly everyday conversation with a cab driver and connects its contents to the formal concept of self-determination. Every challenge, every interaction receives a political, economic, and historical angle.

Most notably, Anmol engages in a bit of comparison and contrast that illuminates the workings of his mind. "Until then," he says, "I had assumed that even if people were unhappy, they always had ways to voice their concerns." Here, we get to see Anmol's naive assumption replaced by a more accurate paradigm. Chechnya works differently from what he's used to; he must adjust his thinking accordingly. Universities expect students to do the same when they meet peers from different lands or read texts that challenge their conception of truth. Hence, when Anmol begins to decipher his own country's situation, he learns of how unequal certain communities have been in his own neighborhood. "As our lives become more insulated, we tend to disregard the narratives of those who don't share our reality." That's a poignant observation, quite pertinent to our current times of information silos and echo chambers. Whether he's connecting the dots between the protest and his sense of identity, or extrapolating a visionary message from a small-scale interaction, Anmol sees the world with bifocal lenses: he's both near-sighted and far-sighted. It's something he shares with Ben Franklin, the inventor of bifocals and the legendary Founding Father of Penn…

Authenticity

OFTEN, AN ESSAY'S GREATEST STRENGTH IS simultaneously its greatest weakness. In this case, we faced a challenge: the story was so much about others, but we needed it to be about Anmol. Luckily, our plucky young author was up for the challenge. By posing the command, "Tell me about yourself" at both the introduction and the conclusion, he taps into a feeling many of us have certainly experienced—especially when asked to write a Common App Essay! What do I say about myself? Where do I begin? The line returns as a refrain providing a beautiful capstone to cement his growth by the end. In the final sentences, Anmol offers a bold, almost cheeky response. We see a newfound confidence in him. The ardent speaker who espouses his life philosophy and ethos here is quite different from the meek, tight-lipped speaker of the first scene. By now, he's recognized how "Boy, things don't work like that. This is the real world." He's been humbled into understanding that his passion for investigation matters only if he's actually helping to improve others' lives.

Hence, when he espouses such inspiring rhetoric ("I want to rekindle our faded historical memory and strengthen collective resolve"), it feels like something of a confession. Anmol is unburdening the load of his earlier reticence. He's a self-aware, determined young soul who's done with the "boring stuff." There are layers beneath the "standard response" (after all, his "identity, too, is constantly transforming"), and we're excited to get to know more of them.

Craft

WE KNOW WHAT YOU'RE THINKING: "BUT this essay isn't all that literary!" Our response: "Does it have to be?"

Anmol's approach makes the most of his talents, which lie primarily in the intellectual realm. For a shy, introverted thinker, it's only natural to go for a style that isn't too showy or fancy. Thus, Anmol employs deceptively simple language and storytelling. The intrigue lies in his use of dialogue (which displays warmth) and academic concepts (which display competence). Take, for example, how charmingly human his little exchange with his uncle feels. Each ellipsis (Um…I'm) mimics his nervous stammering. You can picture him squirming in his shoes while trying to navigate the awkward situation.

Sometimes, Anmol summons unusual vocabulary to capture the specific image: "Learning that almost 1.5 million Chechens lived in a reality they couldn't escape sobered my naivete." Most students would only use *sobered* in reference to substances; if they discussed innocence, they'd use the adjective *naive* but not its noun form. These details truly enliven the prose with an air of maturity. No language choice seems unintentional. Which is exactly as it should be.

EXERCISE

What's one change you'd wish to see in the world in 10 years?
How can you start taking steps toward that ideal right now?
(We encourage you to do this! Right now!)

VOICES FROM WITHIN: HEALING AND EXPRESSION THROUGH POETRY

SARIKA YADAV

Delhi-NCR

University of Pennsylvania

When the brightness of the sun hurts
And you're praying for someone to hold you
through the tornados your mind is spinning
Remember
These roads intersect in your soul

He sat me down on the last step of the white marble staircase. I helplessly reached for the green ribbon on his black suitcase with my tiny hands. "Papa don't go…please don't go." But as he pulled away and walked out the mahogany doors, my wails crescendoed, followed by a downpour of uneasy questions.

"You're too young to understand."

It was the same response every time. Fuel to the flames of my frustration.

I mustered all the emotional and intellectual horsepower of my six-year-old mind to unravel the mystery of my parent's separation.

What did my father want more than to be with his own family? Did he not love my mother anymore? I had to declutter the fragments of my memory, place them in an orderly fashion. I frantically poured my thoughts onto the pages of my diary. Soon, these musings evolved into stories with characters struggling in the same ways. As I devised resolutions to their conflicts, I found peace in some of my own wars. My characters generated scenarios, which I explored through my stories, realizing that every path in life—with my father or without—was not without challenge. Greater acceptance, greater calmness.

But it wasn't enough.

I no longer wanted to confine my words to the pages of my notebook. Even if I had figured things out, I was alone with my thoughts. There was more to each word than the eyes alone could perceive. I wanted to douse every syllable with the musicality of the human voice. This desire blossomed into my love for spoken word poetry. As my emotional awareness strengthened, I garnered the courage to express myself to the world.

Spoken word poetry is a raw expression of its performer's state of mind. It is a synthesis of introspection and expression. It allows me to not only unravel the depths of my own mind, but also connect with empathetic audience members, gain perspective, and accelerate my transformation. Most of my poems start with a heightened sense of chaos and end with clarity. This unintentional structure reflects the self-awareness I gain through the writing and speaking process. Writing about my family helped me understand that sometimes the best thing you can do for your loved ones is to let them go.

I expressed. I connected. I learned that while the problems people face vary, the approaches to overcoming them are curiously similar, stemming from the internal, not the external. My exploration of the nuances of human thought allows me to view the world through new lenses. When I founded my social organization, "Anvesha," I had one goal in mind: to inspire and motivate my peers to reflect profoundly on themselves and contribute positively to their environments. Introspection was the cornerstone of my transformation, and I believed that it would orchestrate theirs as well.

With every Anvesha initiative, from the workshops to the collection of stories from people across the globe, I have endeavored to change mindsets. Today, I have seen students who initially referred to Muslims as "incarnations of the devil" write and perform plays urging members of their societies to treat people from all religious groups the same. Such experiences during my work with Anvesha constantly reinforce to me that meaningful differences on the outside stem from internal realizations.

On my dad, I have come to better understand...he wasn't capable of supporting our dreams when he had unfulfilled ones of his own. Over time, my constant self-reflection has given me the awareness I need to bring order in the face of challenges. I aspire to use this strength I have derived to make a difference in the lives of others, equipping them with the same tools of thought.

Summary

WHAT'S THE STORY ONLY YOU CAN tell? An extremely difficult question—and an extremely critical one. In Sarika's case, however, we had a poet with a challenging past that she was unafraid to confront and share with the world. Tragedy can affect a young person in countless ways. Yet, spotlighting the incident and opening one's heart and mind to the pain are essential to sublimating the experience into something transformative, meaningful, even beautiful. This is precisely what the author does. She recounts her struggle so honestly that we see and even feel her metamorphosis from a terrified child into a maturely compassionate adult. This is how you handle what we call the Divorce/Separation Essay genre. Many other applicants may've suffered a similar experience, but they haven't suffered it the way YOU have. Make us feel invested, as Sarika does.

Values

WHENEVER WE REREAD THIS ESSAY, WE'RE always impressed by Sarika's sophistication of thought and feeling. She values peace and reconciliation, even when she's been shattered by her father's decision to leave the family. One line in particular leaps off the page: "sometimes the best thing you can do for your loved ones is to let them go." Despite the turmoil surrounding her father's departure and her feelings of betrayal, she develops the strength to forgive him, to lay her burden aside and move forward.

She crowns this statement with another, arguably more powerful one in the conclusion: "I have come to better understand...[my dad]

wasn't capable of supporting our dreams when he had unfulfilled ones of his own." What profound awareness! Few teenagers can acknowledge that their parents have growth journeys themselves, and support them in such endeavors despite the pangs of loss. With this poignant paradigm shift, Sarika demonstrates an extremely selfless form of love, giving her blessings to the source of her torment while expecting hardly anything in return. Guaranteed, institutions like Penn—founded on principles of equality and civics—could appreciate such radical compassion.

Perspective

WHO'S THE HERO OF THIS PIECE? Could it perhaps be the diary? It undeniably comes to Sarika's rescue and is responsible for launching her arc of reflection and resurrection. Writing is therapeutic, even talismanic, as it increases the author's "emotional and intellectual horsepower," helping her to organize both her thoughts and feelings. But beyond its capacity to improve her mental fitness, it serves as a wellspring of stories, whose power emerges from their personal roots. In Sarika's own words: "My characters generated scenarios, which I explored through my stories, realizing that every path in life—with my father or without—was not without challenge." Here, we see how introspection inspires evolution, and how, with each scribbled page, there's a corresponding insight that allows her to reframe her perspective. Moreover, by generating characters with similar trials and tribulations, she at least partially dissociates from her conflict, generating the objectivity necessary to gradually discard her baggage.

But the insights don't stop there. We're particularly captivated by her realization that spoken word poetry "is a synthesis of introspection and expression." It requires her to connect both within and without, to expose herself to the tides of judgment. But instead of judgment, she receives catharsis. In everyday parlance, we're tempted to differentiate between introversion and extroversion; Sarika transcends this dichotomy, for as she goes deeper within, she has more to share with her community. And in the process of that sharing, she understands more about herself. Through spoken word, the author has achieved a positive feedback loop that elevates her current state and gives her the tools to write the next chapter of her journey.

In a final stroke of mastery, Sarika demonstrates that she possesses the remarkable capacity to generalize her experience. While many traumatized teens struggle to escape from navel gazing, Sarika identifies a universal principle essential to tackling the seemingly disparate problems others face. They all stem "from the internal, not the external." As Eckhart Tolle and countless mystical traditions of the world state, the world can only change from within.

Authenticity

Any six-year-old would be shattered by the departure of a parent from their home. The author recounts the experience as though it transpired yesterday, including details of the "marble" staircase and "mahogany" door. Her recollection is immaculate, which underscores the impact of this early childhood incident. We must commend Sarika for mustering the courage to embrace her full story; there's no sugarcoating. When she vents that the responses to her innocent questions provided "fuel to the flames of my frustration," it's a perfectly understandable sentiment. This vulnerability forges an immediate bond with the reader, who's eager to witness how this young girl ultimately transforms tragedy into triumph.

Craft

FINALLY, IF THIS ESSAY HAD LACKED craft, it would've fallen flat. The piece is concerned with the sublime power of words, so it must exercise that power with panache. Therefore, Sarika opens with lines of verse, juxtaposing prose with the poetry it inspired. She thus provides the reader with glimpses into her process, how she transmutes pain into art that connects, that heals.

Moreover, the dialogue toward the beginning of the essay further serves to recreate the scene. She tops those cryptic responses with alliteration and several other instances of beautiful language, such as her desire to "douse every syllable with the musicality of the human voice." These aren't cliché, customary phrases; we can't recall the last time we've seen the word "douse" used by a teenager. But that's precisely what gives the writing its luster. By the end, we're enthralled by who Sarika Yadav is and how far she's come. And we have no doubts about how far she'll go.

EXERCISE

What's one incident that causes you discomfort, to whatever extent? Now, if you're willing and able, revisit that incident and list three lessons you can extract from the ordeal.

FROM CONCH SHELLS TO CATHEDRALS: A MUSICAL PILGRIMAGE

SOMIN VIRMANI

Andover

Columbia University

TRUST ME, I LOVE ALL FORMS of music—though my friends *will* try and convince you otherwise. While driving, I routinely queue my favorite film scores, and when feeling particularly enthused at the dinner table, my gastronomic paradise, I play some "delicious" light jazz. Yet, despite the colorful palate of my musical tastes, something always compels me toward Early Music.

Such is quite the curiosity among my friends, who don't relate to the period. I am an organist and vocalist who, almost obsessively, engages with Renaissance and Baroque music, styles preceding the better-known Western Classical era. My friends' passing railleries (my personal favorite: "Are you kidding, Somin?! Beethoven is too experimental for you??") during our Austen-inspired, POC-featuring tea parties have driven me to probe my peculiar relationship with Early Music and with, well, all else.

Upon reflection, I realize that I cherish the overwhelmingly social experience most musical genres foster for me. Whether I'm jamming to Ariana Grande's Billboard hits with my friends, or performing Beethoven's 9th Symphony as the entire concert hall bobs along to its Ode to Joy chorus, these styles help me find a sense of conviviality. They connect me with my fellow musicians, audiences, and friends. My somewhat solitary experience of Early Music, however, seems to channel the opposite.

Perhaps the answer lies in how my first interactions with music—or in essence, sound—were deeply personal. My mom reminisces that as a baby, I sang myself to sleep, alone in the dark, exploring the possibilities of my own voice. Later, I was exposed to the commanding calls of the *shankh*, or conch shell, employed to invoke universal divinity during Hindu religious ceremonies. As a child, I wondered how its primordial bellow heightened my pulse while also imparting the somber notion of sanctity.

Such intimate captivations with sound have established the rhythm of my dance with Early Music, perhaps owing to its origins in religious worship. While playing the organ in my school's chapel, reverberations off of the soaring arches return to me, converging into ethereal, layered harmonies. While singing in the stone cathedrals of Boston, echoes produced by worn marble floors blend into rich audial mosaics. Acutely sensitive to my environment, I consider the effect of these enormous enclosed spaces upon each composition. Moreover, as if to channel the solemnity established by a place of worship, Early Music follows a rather strict methodology that manifests in reverential euphonies. I find the melodies that these compositions birth enrapturing—not unlike that of the *shankh's* bellow.

These outward expressions of Early Music set me on an inward journey. While singing Renaissance motets, I lose myself in the dovetailing voices of my choir. And while playing the organ, even if the pews below me overflow with listeners, I remain consumed by my mental images of fugal lines weaving into a pristine *pas de quatre*. Goosebumps begin to dot my limbs as the organ's formidable vibrations rush through me, directing my attention toward the core of my being. The environment around me dissipates into shadow, my soul under spotlight. Like my infant self, I am free to commune with sound alone, engulfed by nothingness.

Absorbed in this curious solitude, I become one with a sublime universal. I transcend both the collective and the individual; my audience dissolves. All that remains is the intangible, the spiritual—what some would call the divine.

In this moment of profound stillness, I take up space. The wind flowing through each pipe of the organ becomes my own. I permeate my surroundings through the instrument's harmonious roar. My otherwise introverted self sits tall, aspirations soaring upwards. The organ's affirmations fill me with confidence. I am empowered to live boldly.

Oh well, maybe my friends were right. After all, you can like many things, but only one can be your truest love.

Summary

SOME STUDENTS SIMPLY *EXUDE* A BRAND. It simply seeps from their pores, and there's no way to hide it. Thankfully, Somin had no intentions of trying. A first-generation Indian American at one of the country's most prestigious boarding schools, with achievements in the arts and public health, he possessed clear potential. More specifically, he had a niche interest—the organ—for which he gallivanted the world as part of a chamber ensemble. We quickly concluded that this unusual talent and obsession must be the centerpiece of his essay. Music represented something entirely personal and transcendent for Somin, which nicely complemented the more stereotypical aspects of his profile. His distinct love for obscure "Early Music," if presented gracefully, could even inspire readers normally alienated by such genres (it was an activity certainly appreciated at Columbia, where the arts and humanities receive special attention amid the cosmopolitan sophistication of New York City!). Hence, we always tell students to focus on specifics: being true to your individual experience paradoxically helps others relate to you.

In the particular is contained the universal.

—James Joyce

Values

ONE PERVASIVE MYTH ABOUT AMERICAN UNIVERSITIES is that they only want the so-called "well-rounded" student. People assume that hyper-focused, hyper-specialized scholars may as well seek the more academically oriented UK, where changing your major is more difficult, and extracurricular activities less important. Promoters of this myth should review the Common Data Set for elite American schools, which always cite "Talent/Ability" as a "Very Important" factor. Usually, the only way to become accomplished at a task or skill is to master it through time, effort, and patience. Somin's passion for Early Music, through the organ, revealed something deeper about his character. He was bold enough not to care that it was unpopular. He was committed enough to stay the course. He was rigorous enough to know all the history and technical details. Synesthetic phrases like "layered harmonies" and "audial mosaics" reflect a musician who's thoroughly dedicated to his craft.

Even better, he was rooted in his ancestral culture. Our initial question had been, "Why Western music and not traditional Indian sounds?" This was a kid who refused to be placed into either box; he embraced the influence of his current home, America, while also appreciating the heritage of the Hindu *shankh*. Moreover, he unites the two ideas through the theme of spiritual transcendence, and as a result presents himself as both open to the diversity of an elite American campus and sufficiently grounded to add something to it. And dare someone argue that he's mired in the more irrational or sentimental aspects of religion, he couches the whole discussion in scientific terms and music theory ("strict methodology"). The result? We're impressed.

Perspective

AS WE SAY REPEATEDLY, ELITE UNIVERSITIES want students who are thinkers. Somin was a true intellectual. While remaining in tune with his emotions, he never forgot to exercise his brain. You can see it in how the entire essay is written in reflective mode: "Our Austen-inspired, POC-featuring tea parties have driven me to probe my peculiar relationship with Early Music and with, well, all else." He wants to understand why he thinks and feels the way he does. Each paragraph is an introspective revelation, distinguishing his solitary experience with Early Music from the social elements of other genres. The narrative is a fact-finding mission—a scientific inquiry into emotional states, intercultural musical traditions, and most poignantly, selfhood. This is what all true personal essays do. The transitions in thought need not occur as a single epiphany toward the end. They can and should be woven organically into the entire journey.

Authenticity

AN ESSAY ON A TOPIC LIKE music can only work if your obsessiveness can actually compel your reader to connect with you. Cerebral writers like Somin typically struggle to offer sufficient warmth to make us care about THEM, not just their offbeat passions.

Hence, when it came to the actual essay idea, one of the most interesting quirks that arose was Somin's odd ritual of hosting those "Austen-inspired, POC-featuring tea parties" with his friends. Our initial mental image was of a diverse circle of teens dressed in 18th-century garb, sipping from porcelain cups with their pinkies up. How many kids his age did stuff like that? From this to jazz and the *shankh*, it was clear that we were dealing with an old soul. That was a brand! Why not lean into that with a little levity?

Self-deprecation, through humor, is among the most effective ways of becoming relatable. So, we see our snobbish author crack a line at his own expense: "Are you kidding, Somin?! Beethoven is too experimental for you??" Even his old-fashioned friends are hipper than he! Someone who isn't self-aware can't express the inner security to be so flippantly candid. By contrast, Somin is willing to deflate his high-minded persona without completely undermining it. Inserted carefully into the narrative, this hilarious moment helps ground an otherwise pretentious discussion.

And what's more, Somin makes it clear that he isn't solely into the esoteric stuff. He likes "Ariana Grande's Billboard hits" just as much as the next kid. These brief, seemingly minor admissions produce a significant effect on the reader's perception of our author: he's an immensely talented soul, but ultimately, he's one of us.

Craft

AGAIN, WE WERE LUCKY IN THAT Somin came to us with an already clear, finely honed sense of literary voice. His intellectual character shone through distinct word choices like "railleries" and "conviviality" used by few teens—or even adults! Every intricate description ("primordial bellow heightened my pulse while also imparting the somber notion of sanctity"), every example of advanced grammar ("I am an organist and vocalist who, almost obsessively, engages...")

showcases a command over literary turns of phrase. There's a sharpness throughout each sentence that carefully avoids bland generalities. He offers no platitudes, only specifics. And thoughtful language choices —like the italics in "though my friends *will* try and convince you otherwise"—speak volumes about the cheeky, authentic human being wielding the pen.

Indeed, Somin's choice to frame the entire essay around a simple question posed during a tea party encapsulates boldness and depth of thought. As readers, we're brought into his world, his mental and emotional existence. From the first line, the speaker makes it clear that this won't be your conventional narrative—it's not really a "story" at all—for this is far from a conventional student. Through an expository essay written primarily in present tense, we actually learn a great deal about Somin's background nonetheless. He shows us that you don't need to offer a straightforward chronology of events to make a reader connect with your context. By the time you reach the end, with that fun final line riffing on the idea of monogamy, you've been convinced that this is one multifaceted chap you need to meet.

EXERCISE

Do you have any quirky hobbies or interests that few others are into? Why are you so passionate about them? Use this space to defend your passion.

THE ETHICAL RICKSHAW RIDE: A JOURNEY IN SITUATIONAL ETHICS

PRANAY GUPTA

Delhi-NCR

Cornell University

"70 रूपये *(70 RUPEES)*," SAYS THE auto-rickshaw driver as we arrive outside my house. We had originally agreed on 50.

My mind begins to warm up. *What should I do?*

Economically, I must act in accordance with Adam Smith's conception of self-interest and pay him the lower price. As a rational consumer, this will maximize my economic utility. However, economics also dictates that aggregate human welfare must be increased. I begin to question whether paying the driver an extra 20 rupees from my position of privilege will increase human welfare and serve as the economically sound decision.

My mind starts to jog slowly. *But are his actions moral?*

The consequentialist in me, having noticed a picture of the driver's family of seven posted inside, justifies his actions from a position of sympathy. My mind reasons that regardless of the driver's actions, the outcome would be an improved livelihood for his family. With that, I reach for the wad of 20-rupee notes in my pocket to draw one out—until the texture of that 20-rupee note between my fingers sours my idealistic conception of serving social justice. I cannot deny the stark reality that I have just been blatantly lied to and scammed.

In this moment, I am reminded of one of Kant's moral imperatives: one must act according to the maxim that one would be satisfied with if it were universal law. I cannot bring myself to stand for a society in which lying and scamming, regardless of the motivations, are the universal norms; I cannot stand for the erosion of our social fabric. A mark of civilization is the respect for contracts. This was a verbal contract.

My mind gains steam. I glance at a poster of a Lord Rama displayed on the back of the vehicle. *Almighty deity, do you have the answer?*

I rack my brain for the countless nuggets of Hindu philosophy that my father, an ardent follower of the Bhagavad Gita, has imparted to me throughout my 17 years. My mind begins listing the virtues that Lord Krishna prescribed, categorizing the driver as a demonic character incapable of honesty. But is it really "demonic" to want to feed one's family, *a la* Jean Valjean? Isn't helping others in line with *dana* (giving) and a key component of one's *dharma* (duty)?

My musing is halted by the visibly disgruntled driver demanding that I pay up. In a daze, I finally hand him the 20-rupee note and begin to walk away, still unsure of what I should have done.

In a preoccupied state, I plod toward the door, pausing after each step. My mind, meanwhile, is running at full throttle. *Economic self-interest or human welfare? Smith or Marshall? Consequentialism or deontology? Mill or Kant? Individualism or collectivism?*

Like a wild stallion, my mind loves to run, untamed. It particularly relishes challenges of situational ethics, such as this little escapade with the fateful rickshaw driver. Initially, I was frustrated by my inability to settle on a single perspective. But now, I appreciate that there is always some other way of looking at things, some other theory to consider, some other question to ask.

Although my mind often divorces me from my immediate surroundings and makes me lose myself in thought, this process helps me gain a better understanding of myself and the world around me. From refining my views on normative ethics every time I see a beggar on the street to forcing me to distinguish between nationalism and patriotism at the first note of the national anthem in the movie theater, my mind enables me to extract wisdom, my ultimate purpose.

As I wait for the elevator door to open, my mind is at complete ease for a split second, knowing the next ethical dilemma is right around the corner...

Summary

NOW, FOR A VERY DIFFERENT PIECE. At Athena, we're big on heart. We're big on inspiration. We're big on motivation. However, there's something appealing about combining heart with raw intellectual horsepower. In the following essay, you'll witness a young mind attempting to bring order to the chaotic soup of existence, arranging information into a semblance of structure. This is who Pranay is. He thinks...and thinks. He loves it—and he's good at it. He ponders a dilemma not from two angles, but from multiple. And this is a skill prized by admissions departments, for it's essentially what academics do: arrange information into structures, building on the foundations laid by past scholars for posterity, so we as a civilization can continue our journey toward knowledge and self-actualization.

Values

WE PERSONALLY LOVE THE ACADEMIC DEPTH that permeates this writing. It's truly inspiring to observe a teenager so effortlessly open with a discussion on the influential economist Adam Smith. Here's a budding scholar who studies economic philosophy not to pass an exam (although from his academic record, he has no issue with that!), but to live what Socrates would call a more examined life. To Pranay, every precept he reads in a book is a guideline for action, and he's grappling with the question of which to apply where. Knowing when to do what, when to be what, is the hallmark of wisdom, and the author explicitly states in the conclusion that this is his ultimate purpose. He displays a maturity of thought well beyond his years, to the inevitable delight of admissions officers and future mentors.

Beyond that, Pranay demonstrates the capacity to approach truth through multiple channels. He tacitly acknowledges that a single theory cannot suffice in lighting the path of wisdom; he must seek counsel from all the historical greats, from across disciplinary boundaries (including his own cultural context of India!). Moreover, he subscribes to the maxim "strong opinions, loosely held," wholeheartedly critiquing his own point of view. He isn't concerned with maintaining a half-baked "consistency," and instead recognizes that education is the progressive discovery of one's own ignorance, as Will Durant famously stated. So, in his pursuit of true education, Pranay keeps questioning his conclusions, never satisfied with conventional responses. He wants to know, without a shred of doubt, what's the right thing to do, and he's willing to look anywhere for the answer. Even the *Bhagavad Gita*.

Perspective

IN THIS CASE, PERSPECTIVE OVERLAPS CONSIDERABLY with Values. Pranay's insights stem from the realization that "being good" is difficult, for different frameworks point in different directions. Which one is right? Is each right in a particular situation? If so, which situation is *this*? Should I simply take an average? A weighted average, perhaps? Pranay impresses his readers not only by discussing disparate disciplines, but also by highlighting contrasting opinions within the same discipline. There is both individual and collective utility maximization, but also Immanuel Kant's categorical imperative, none of which completely agree with each other! Then Pranay goes on to quote the *Bhagavad Gita* (as did J. Robert Oppenheimer and Indiana Jones) and *Les Miserables* in the same paragraph, again underscoring that he's an intellectual heavyweight. This is precisely the kind of student that institutions like Cornell wish to foster on their campuses.

Authenticity

TO ROUND OUT THE DISCUSSION, IT'S important to highlight that although this is a concept-heavy essay, plenty of vulnerability still shines through. First of all, Pranay's entire story is centered on a problem that isn't just intellectual but also emotional. He deeply desires to be compassionate yet fair. Hence, he isn't the picture-perfect Do-Gooder who does what he thinks he's supposed to. A less-mature goody two-shoes would simply give up the money and not think twice about it. But Pranay has nuance, complexity. He directly acknowledges that "I have just been blatantly lied to and scammed."

Deeper, he freely admits his shortcomings—particularly that most difficult of admissions, "I don't know." Even after all the back and forth, he remains at square one. But he's okay with that. For there's no end to the life of the mind; it's a journey on which the traveler gains a little more wisdom with each step. And that's the journey Pranay is committed to. He'll certainly stumble along the way, but by the end of the piece, the reader has no doubt that he'll pick himself up and continue scaling his mountain.

Craft

AND THAT BRINGS US TO CRAFT. The first line of the submission isn't even English. This was a deliberate stylistic choice, which immediately places the reader in another setting. We ain't in Kansas anymore, Dorothy! This is no Ivy League discussion group; we're in the real world with real concerns, and we're gonna have to make real decisions with real consequences. Yes, this is how deeply we pondered the very first sentence!

The motif that runs through the entire piece is also noteworthy. Pranay's mind is personified, incorporating elements of both a horse and a locomotive. It warms up, gains steam, and presses forward. The single-line paragraphs between arguments add a creative overlay to help us visualize how Pranay navigates the world and perceives himself. He is a thought athlete, and thinking is serious business. No wonder we chose to go with a single moment in time (what literature folks call a "slice of life") instead of an extended narrative of events. The use of present tense instead of past gives Pranay's whole essay an air of urgency. Everything seems to be happening in real time—including the whirring of his brain. And with this dense, delightful, multi-layered dialogue, Pranay successfully signals to universities that he's ready to hit the ground running!

EXERCISE

When have you felt conflicted about a decision? What are the arguments for and against? What are the inspirations for those arguments? Weighing them all, what path would you choose?

The Road Less Conformed: A Tale of Bikes, Clay, and Breaking Molds

MRITUNJAY BOSE

Delhi-NCR

Princeton University

ONE MOMENT I WAS ADMIRING THE SHINY BMW RS1250 motorbike. Next, I was clutching its rear handles for dear life! Delhi rushed past, blurry. But it was hard to ignore the turning heads. These looks had a language of their own; they were what had gotten me here.

★ ★ ★

"Buddha hai kya?"
"Are you sixteen or sixty?"
"Why don't you play basketball anymore, Mritunjay? Oops, you can't."

While my classmates uploaded selfies on Instagram, I stared at X-rays. MRIs of spines. I was the only sixteen-year-old regularly hunched in the orthopedics department. After the doctor's suspicions of microdiscectomy

95

proved correct ("at such a young age too, tch"), I began my toxic relationship with pain. Turned away from the basketball team I had called family for four years and every athletic club at school, I found myself at the doors of the Culinary Club. As its only male member, I was prepared for fresh jibes. Instead, I was handed a recipe, ingredients, and a smiling thumbs up.

Left to my own devices, I could tinker with sauces or chop vegetables *a la* Masterchef. I could spend hours giving a box of ingredients the flavor of my imagination. It could be anything. With no one to judge me here, I could be anyone. Clad in a frilly apron at a cluttered table, I was the picture of contentment. Not bad for Instagram, eh?

My classmates had different ideas.

"Ladki hai kya?"
"Are you a woman?"
"All this pots-and-pans business is for girls, bro."
One space. One hobby. One niche where I was comfortable. Should I give it up too? Chop off bits of my personality to be acceptable to the typical "bro"?

That night when I was asked to help out in the kitchen, I almost said no. But my aunt had come over and my mother could use the extra help. As I puttered around the kitchen - reluctant for the first time - my aunt gushed:

"An all-female biker gang, Rohini, can you believe it? They're called Bikerni or something..."

I googled them. In a country that still harbors not-so-subtle gender stereotypes, Bikerni was an uncompromising beacon of feminism, riding unapologetically through the streets on their Harleys. I pondered long and hard before my trembling fingers mustered enough courage to hit send.

"Hi, my name is Mritunjay. Could I ask you a question?"

To my three-page-long e-mail, the leader of Bikerni extended a one-line proposition.

"Catch a ride with us?"

★ ★ ★

As I rode behind Krishna ma'am, the shiny BMW continued to attract disapproving stares. When we finally paused for fuel, I burst out.

"But don't they bother you? The stares? The comments?"

The leader of Bikerni kicked the bike back to life before answering.

"Who cares what others think? If you enjoy it, do it. An all-women biker gang is not an everyday sight, but that is what sets us apart. Empowers us. We could do what society expects us to. But, we wouldn't be doing what we love. We wouldn't be us."

Even as my back protested against the ride, I smiled. Maybe there was merit to being called "old." For all the pain I'd suffered, I'd stopped taking the little things for granted. Perhaps there was pride in being called "feminine." My respect for women doubled every time I saw my mother successfully navigating a full-time job and a family. It manifested itself in my enjoyment of all things beautiful and strong, in the one-room where I could be unapologetically me.

Although the world exists in binaries, it's always the differences that make us unique. I may not conform to binaries, the 0 and 1, the black and white. But exploring the grey is what makes me unique. I could either choose to be ashamed of it. Or I could be empowered by it.

The bumpy ride jarred my bones and shifted something within. I made my decision.

Summary

NOW, MRITUNJAY WAS ONE OF THOSE rare Indian male STEM students who possessed a genuinely interesting profile. Instead of physics or chemistry or engineering—all broad categories—he chose a specific niche: material science. How many kids are studying that? Additionally, Mritunjay had a love for the culinary arts—again, not terribly stereotypical for an Indian male Stemmie—plus a debilitating back condition that had led others to label him as "old." Sounded like a story. But things got even better when he started getting into motorcycles and conducting free repairs for his community. Even *even* better, he'd connected with a crew of all-women bikers who welcomed him into their fold. There was such ripe material here; all we had to do was harvest it. The result was Mritunjay's own spin on *Zen and the Art of Motorcycle Maintenance*—a high concept that readers would surely remember.

Values

ONE OF THE FIRST THINGS THAT strikes you about Mritunjay is his sensitivity. He's compassionate toward women throughout the essay because he was raised right. Inspired by the feminine energy surrounding him—"But my aunt had come over and my mother could use the extra help"—he'd cultivated an appreciation of how they, too, feel marginalized by society. The key is that, unlike many young male authors, he avoids the trap of mansplaining or ignoring women's perspectives. He gives them names ("Krishna Ma'am"), a place to speak ("If you enjoy it, do it. An all-women biker gang isn't an everyday sight, but that's what sets us apart. Empowers us"). The women come off as real characters instead of props to support his claim of caring about the cause.

In the process, we come to respect Mritunjay. He seems to recognize that his lived experience isn't the same, just similar in many ways. Thus, he has much to learn from these unusual mentors. Readers want to see such openness to growth. They don't want to see negativity and whining. Had this been a woe-is-me, the-world-is-out-to-get-me, I'm-in-pain kind of a narrative, it would've been a total drag. Instead, we get to see a young man with a refreshing set of qualities, someone who'll no doubt get along well with the diversity—gender, sexuality, physical ability—that abounds on elite American campuses.

Perspective

THE BEST ESSAYS ALMOST ALWAYS INCLUDE a bit of social commentary. Here, it's subtle, but certainly meaningful. As an Indian male feminist, Mritunjay places himself squarely against the prevailing social mores of his parents' country. Growing up at least partly in the States, his birthplace, he's a perpetual outsider in India. But insight typically derives from having sufficient detachment to observe people and society from a distance and critique what one sees. Most kids lack this ability, whether they're originally from their local community or not. Lines like "In a country that still harbors not-so-subtle gender stereotypes, *Bikerni* was an uncompromising beacon of feminism, riding unapologetically through the streets on their Harleys" highlight the author's penetrating analysis. They reflect that Mritunjay is aware and unafraid to acknowledge the disparities he witnesses. We always say that the willingness to offer your own culture tough love is a sign of both intellectual and emotional maturity. It takes perspective and courage. So, when Mritunjay calls himself "grey" toward the end ("I may not conform to binaries, the 0 and 1, the black and white"), he demonstrates the capacity for nuance, which is essential for the kinds of academic environments he seeks.

Authenticity

WOW, LOOK AT HOW MUCH THIS guy puts himself out there! The jokes keep coming, like clockwork. All this was by design, of course. We recognized that Mritunjay's exuberant, energetic personality needed to be captured on paper. It was a characteristic that distinguished him among his more typically reserved peers. If he can laugh at himself through lines like "Why don't you play basketball anymore, Mritunjay? Oops, you can't or asides like "Not bad for Instagram, eh?" then perhaps we, too, can laugh with him. Or at least smile. Either way, you feel drawn to such a persona. You want to root for him. Anyone who can own something seemingly negative like being "old" is unstoppable. By the end, Mritunjay has become rather unfazed by the quizzical looks. He's (mostly) conquered an ongoing insecurity. Who couldn't relate to that?

Craft

AS YOU CAN SEE, MRITUNJAY IS no literary writer, per se. Unlike some of his peers, he leans not on fancy sentence structure and mellifluous diction but rather on simple, straightforward language delivered with clarity. Our framing device in the very first paragraph, beginning with the shiny BMW RS1250, gets the reader interested—and invested.

We want to know more about his mysterious bike ride through the Delhi streets, so we keep reading. The callback near the final line—"The bumpy ride jarred my bones and shifted something within. I made my decision"—brings us closure. Similarly, the partly humorous, partly serious use of dialogue throughout gives voice to speakers seen and unseen. Because it so accurately mirrors how teenagers actually talk, we believe it. Mritunjay has taken us into his world. Which works all the better when we see that Krishna Ma'am speaks with the calm authority of greater age and wisdom. When you paint a full picture of the world around you, we indeed believe that you've been embraced by an all-women Indian biker gang!

EXERCISE

Can you think of any times when a personal failing, ailment, or circumstance made you feel inferior to others? How did you learn to confront or embrace your situation?

From Stubble to Strength: A Journey in Antifragility

RAGHAV PARDASANI

Delhi-NCR

The University of Chicago

CHAPTER 1: THE MASTER

The *treasure* lay in a brown corrugated box.

My entry into the cavernous basement sent a vortex of dust into the stagnant air. As the room illuminated, I saw a cardboard box with an almost-illegible "stubble" scrawled across it. I wheezed. The grit down here was nothing compared to the toxic gray haze enveloping Delhi. One reason for this pollution was the "ritual" of stubble burning, in which North-Indian farmers burn rice husk to clear their fields. Now, I was seeking another use for that very stubble.

I removed two golden strands from the box and placed them on either palm, so they were perfectly aligned. I started to braid the strands to form a supple rope. Despite my efforts, the product looked terrible!

Fortunately, I came across Pramod, a farmer in our neighborhood, who offered guidance. "You made this?" he inquired, a smile tugging at his lips. "It needs a lot of work." Pramod then sat down and started to weave rope. From positioning his hands to rubbing the straws, Pramod was meticulous at every step. I stared, mesmerized.

"Could you teach me how to do it?"

"I can," Pramod began, "but only once you forget *your* way of doing it."

Now that I learned how to make the ropes, the next step was to make a bag.

When I finished, the threads were loose and the stitching messy. I began to doubt myself. And as always, this stirred up the entrance of Tughlaq.

CHAPTER 2: FIRE AND WIND

Muhammad Bin Tughlaq was an infamous Indian ruler, whose policies of shifting the capital and introducing his token currency led to economic chaos and the ultimate disintegration of his kingdom.

Owing to his unsuccessful ventures that had serious ramifications, Tughlaq had become a representation of my self-aggrandizing-fixed mindset. When I couldn't lead my team to qualify for the Wharton Investment Competition earlier this year, Tughlaq amplified my fears and insecurities.

You failed. You are a failure.

Now, as I worked on the bag, Tughlaq re-emerged, in full bloom.

Leave the bag—you are not an artist.

However, I wanted to try once more. Pramod's words had moved me—he didn't just teach me how to make the ropes, but also how I could *learn* to do something by *unlearning* flawed techniques. In the next bag I wove, there remained flaws, but I began to see them as improvements that hadn't been made yet.

A new understanding dawned on me: the best way to deal with failure is not to repel it, but to embrace it—to unlearn, relearn, and finally become *antifragile*. Unlike robustness, antifragility does not signify withstanding the challenges, but thriving as a result of them:

When a wind attempts to extinguish a small flame, it grows into a bonfire.

CHAPTER 3: BAG'S STORY

Guess who I am?

I am one of the stubble bags that Raghav created. At first, I was very poorly constructed. Every time I stood up, there were forces that swept me off my feet. I felt like Forky from *Toy Story 4*, whose tendency to scuttle towards trash was comparable to my inevitable collapse.

But then, I underwent a transformation. My stitching was tightened and my hair trimmed—it was almost as though I were reborn. Through a constant state of adaptation, I strive to be of a higher utility to all those around me.

My creation is a testament to Raghav's new guiding philosophy to become *antifragile*, but the presence of Tughlaq still bothers him: Tughlaq became the Madeline Wuntch to Raghav's Ray Holt—insulting but unknowingly refining him.

Far from being a detriment, Tughlaq's unpleasant yet sometimes honest words are responsible for Raghav's antifragility. He is the flame, and Tughlaq the wind that threatens to put him out but never succeeds. And with every gust, Raghav emerges stronger and brighter.

Summary

OUR BUDDY RAGHAV WAS AN UNDERSTANDABLY nervous self-doubter. He was a Standard Strong Indian Male economics applicant (a crowded pool) with no immediate hook to place him in the "shoo-in" category. Luckily, he had something interesting up his sleeve: a project no other student seemed to be pulling off. It involved the arts as well as environmentalism, a burgeoning movement in a rapidly developing nation. Naturally, instead of shying away from Raghav's feelings, we encouraged him to lean into them! Why not turn your perceived weakness into a strength? Why not give them a spin? Isn't that what budding entrepreneurs do? Most applicants are too afraid to present themselves in such a manner, but it's one of the best ways to connect with your reader. That, matched with a creative, thought-provoking approach, can win over even the toughest AO.

Values

ONE OF THE FIRST THINGS YOU'LL notice about Raghav is his genuine care for the world. At the start, he recognizes a local problem that disturbs him: stubble burning. And instead of merely complaining or passing the buck, he decides to take action. His well-intentioned social project reflects compassion for nature and her inhabitants.

But that's just where the epic saga begins. We read further and learn that despite intending to fashion the bags, Raghav faces a significant knot in his plans: weaving the material is hard! Again, instead of merely giving up, he seeks help from someone who's already mastered the skill. He keeps trying, tuning out the tempting negativity of Emperor Tughlaq in his head (note the cultural rootedness!). Universities know that students will face challenges at college—and beyond. No matter how smart you are, how talented, how capable, you'll sometimes find yourself outside your element. Raghav shows that he'll adapt just fine to being a small fish in a big pond. That growth mindset—a concept proposed by psychologist Carol Dweck—underlies the antifragility that infuses his character. Proposed by the economist and philosopher Nassim Nicholas Taleb, "antifragility" is the capacity for becoming stronger with increased strain—as opposed to being simply resilient.

If Raghav is capable of interweaving such intellectual ideas from diverse fields, including the historical figure of Tughlaq, he just might embody the American liberal-arts ideal. Students are expected to be scholars in the truest sense of the word: intellectuals who live the life of the mind. That is, lifelong learners. And that just happens to be a foundational pillar of the institution Raghav now attends, The University of Chicago. How coincidental.

Perspective

THROUGHOUT THIS PIECE, RAGHAV PONDERS THE role of failure as both an inhibiting and empowering force. Of course, many students write about failure. It's in fact the second official Common App Essay prompt: "Recount a time when you faced a challenge, setback, or failure." Many of the other prompts also ask something similar regarding how you might've changed your thought process or perspective. No one's expecting you to reinvent the wheel; what's far more important is offering a take that's specific to YOU. In this case, Raghav recognizes that his "self-aggrandizing" mirrors that of Tughlaq, whose "unsuccessful ventures" had "serious ramifications." Through comparison and contrast, Raghav can gain an accurate picture of where he stands. Tughlaq is a mental boogeyman he must defeat. And his weapon of choice? "Unlearn[ing]" and "relearn[ing]." Willful "transformation." Raghav reinvents himself, observing that "He is the flame, and Tughlaq the wind that threatens to put him out but never succeeds." After all, fire needs oxygen to burn. "And with every gust, Raghav emerges stronger and brighter." It's not a rejection of Tughlaq, but rather an embrace. He welcomes this apparent enemy as a paradoxical friend. Do most kids possess that kind of maturity?

Authenticity

AS WE'VE SEEN WITH OTHER ESSAYS, high-minded discussions can easily fall flat if they're not down to earth. Here, we've got psychological and philosophical theories, niche historical figures, and grand, sweeping statements of wisdom. What makes it all palatable is how Raghav presents it. For each pretentious element, there's a reference to pop culture, like Forky from *Toy Story 4* or Wuntch and Holt from *Brooklyn Nine-Nine*. It makes no difference whether you've watched these works; simple passing knowledge is enough to perceive what he's doing. This author is a real kid, with flesh and blood. He has normal interests. And he's secure enough to make light of himself.

Where most applicants would never admit imperfection, he centers the entire narrative around that very idea! The rhetoric of admissions officers may seem to favor candidates who present their "best selves," but most students misinterpret this sentiment—the most accurate definition of "best" is "always getting better." It can be most endearing for a Type-A achiever to admit a real shortcoming. That reflects profound maturity. For teens who've always been good at everything, they may be fine discussing their accomplishments, but they often struggle to address their worst fear: ineptitude. Raghav, in contrast, tackles it head on. He lets us into his psyche, presenting the scene with Pramod in the most authentic manner. The subtle humor of "a smile tugging at his lips" speaks volumes in just six words. Deeper, though, the gentle, poignant moment of Pramod telling Raghav to humble himself speaks even more. Our protagonist is willing to become a student to someone below his socioeconomic status. There's no pride or arrogance in that. Bruce Lee famously spoke of how one must empty their "cup" to be filled with the water of his teachings; Pramod is the *guru*, and Raghav his *shishya*.

Craft

THE FORM OF AN ESSAY MUST reflect the perspective of its author. Where Raghav was anxious and all over the place personally, it made perfect sense to convey that waywardness through the content and form. Indeed, the busyness of all the ideas and sections threatened to unravel the fabric of this zany Frankenstein of a piece. Luckily, the common thread was always clear. We find that the three-part structure, complete with headings, serves three distinct stages of Raghav's growth journey. The inclusion of so many allusions and references provides the reader with several images that weave together instead of pulling apart. Even the unique third-person perspective of the final chapter, told through Forky's eyes, provides a sort of reflection on how far Raghav has come—all while avoiding the cliché of revealing the Pivot and subsequent philosophical outpouring in first-person perspective. The result is fresh, intriguing. It's so left field that you don't expect it, but welcome it nonetheless. All loose threads of the narrative tie together, and you feel that this section of Raghav's journey is complete, like the notorious stubble bag. You hope to keep reading for the next.

EXERCISE

Think back to a time when you learned that you were terrible at some task, skill, or activity. How did it feel to be incompetent? Did you learn something from the (humbling) experience?

Red Stains and Revelations: Confronting Menstrual Stigma through Art

NANDITA KAUL

Jaipur

Columbia University

"YOU ARE NOT ALLOWED TO ENTER the temple," my mother announced.

This was the lowest point of an already terrible week, which had started when blood seeped through my school skirt. Horrified, I scurried to the restroom. No one was supposed to know I was on my period - especially not the boys. Changing into black sweatpants, I attempted to unobtrusively slink back to class, but a male friend caught me: "Why aren't you wearing your school skirt?" I stammered, "I... I sat on paint during art class." So embarrassing! Could the week get any worse?

Apparently, yes. I had looked forward to a family celebration at the temple that Tuesday, until Mom kindly reminded me that I was banned from entry. I thought back to the day this monthly ordeal started. I was bewildered that the temple, the kitchen, and dadi's (grandmother's) room were all off-limits. I had no idea what a "cycle" was, but understood that it made me impure.

As my family departed for the temple, I questioned God, frustrated: "If you made me this way, why can't I enter your abode? Why must I be treated as a lesser being because of a natural function of my body?!"

I would not let this go. I even angrily related my experiences with women I worked with at Satyam, my feminist social service initiative, and discovered that they had their own issues on the matter. They used cloth pads because they were too ashamed to purchase menstrual products, and had to secretly wash these cloth pads because of the stigma. Given this unhygienic practice, they experienced chronic reproductive health problems. I was stunned: this stigma affected not only psychological health, as in my case, but also the physical health of millions of underprivileged Indian women.

This was the tipping point. I had to show everyone that menstruation must not be shamed, but celebrated as a life-giving phenomenon. As always when facing an inner conflict, I went to my other temple, one that did not bar me from entering: the art studio. For me, art had always been a personal medium of expression. It was an instrument to express my own ideas and emotions, and understand myself better.

This time, no matter how much I painted, something was missing. My experience at Satyam had taught me that menstrual stigma was not just something *I* faced; it was a *collective* issue. My paintings represented my own frustration, but I longed to capture the suffering of the collective experience. Without doing so, how could I demonstrate the pervasiveness of the stigma and its disastrous consequences?

Desiring to understand others' experiences, I sent a survey to my classmates about menstruation. I cringed as I hit "send" - they would no doubt laugh or be disgusted. However, the next morning, I had fifty responses! I supplemented these responses with stories from the women at Satyam to create my first "crowd-sourced art installation": drenched in red, I stood, surrounded by a constellation of stories that showed the viewer that across India, and even inside a supposedly elite school, girls had to hide their pads inside clenched fists as boys snickered immaturely. I stood not as one individual, but as a representation of all the women seeking a change.

The installation was a turning point; it started a conversation about menstrual stigma at my school, which is the first step to erasing it. I even took pictures of my installation to women at Satyam, which inspired conversations in the village panchayat (council).

More than anything, I experienced a personal transformation - not only did I gain the confidence to stand up to social wrongs, I also learned that art has a curious power to transform cultural discourse. Art makes the unseen seen, forces us to confront unpleasant truths, and inspires progress. I hope to use this, and develop other colors in my palette, to further serve society.

Summary

TELL YOUR STORY FEARLESSLY. THIS IS the advice we constantly share with young writers, and when they dig deep and find the courage to open their hearts, the essays sing. Nandita succeeds in this effort; as a result, we see a fiery determination to question regressive elements of India's status quo. More importantly, she acts decisively to provide an alternative for herself and countless other young women. The reader is left spellbound, convinced that this genuine Do-Gooder will no doubt spearhead positive change in her communities for decades to come. And this is precisely the kind of student elite institutions seek while building their classes each year. They don't want the ones who play it safe; they want the changemakers!

Values

PURITY IS A CONTROVERSIAL SUBJECT, ONE that has led to the marginalization of communities for ages. Nandita's values stem from inclusivity, from honoring the diverse gifts of individuals instead of subscribing to limiting notions of virtue. As she's banned from more and more spaces during her period, her exasperation only grows. Increasingly, she wishes to reform the very ideological institution that constrains her and others. A poignant moment arises when she asks God how a perfectly natural bodily function can be unholy. Her indignation channels a frustration expressed by millions of girls living in conservative societies—not just in India but around the world.

"I would not let this go." Again, we cherish the simple, declarative statements that say so much in so few words. Here's a young rebel refusing to trod the customary path, to play by the rules outlined by her ancestors. And through her leadership in thought and action, she proceeds to provide a voice to countless other women. Nandita's initiative also highlights another element of her character: she's comfortable interacting with women of all demographic backgrounds, from her current school to the village panchayat. A teenager capable of empathizing with those from diverse walks of life is no doubt impressive to admissions officers, who themselves are used to essays from would-be Do-Gooders that treat disadvantaged populations as mere props to make the author look good. Nandita, instead, is the ideal sort of Do-Gooder. She demonstrates the openness of heart and mind to engage positively and productively with eclectic campus peers. Surely, she'll help others find a community and home.

Perspective

NANDITA UNDERGOES A TRANSFORMATION WHEN SHE realizes that her issue isn't individual; it's almost universal: "my experience at Satyam had taught me that menstrual stigma was not just something *I* faced; it was a *collective* issue." Moreover, many others have it even worse, for they lack the resources to address menstruation in a safe, healthy way. At this point, the problem becomes not just about her, but about her entire sisterhood, for whom she now assumes responsibility. She recognizes that the stigma affects both psychological and physical health, which ignites her wish to help generate solutions on a societal scale.

And, of course, the other hero of the essay is Art. For Nandita, art is a haven, a temple that doesn't judge. And through her "Art Collective," she manages to compile more responses than she could've ever imagined. Soon, she presents an installation piece that captures the struggles of countless young women—an aesthetic "class action suit" of sorts to promote positive changes in mindset and policy. Here, Nandita provides wise insights on the age-old relationship between art and activism. Art isn't just about visual appeal; it's also about communicating unspoken truths and inspiring a better tomorrow. And, no doubt, the committee reviewing Nandita's profile was convinced that she wouldn't stop until everyone in her community of young women witnessed that tomorrow.

Authenticity

AGAIN, THERE ISN'T A SINGLE MOMENT of vulnerability; rather, it permeates the entire discussion. The topic of menstruation itself is taboo, so by revealing her unadulterated thoughts, Nandita welcomes both ridicule and castigation. Indignant, she consults the Almighty with a lucid—and powerful—question: "Why must I be treated as a lesser being because of a natural function of my body?!" Few students are willing to be so bold as to doubt their creator in an essay; most avoid the subject of religion altogether, the way they avoid politics and sexuality (which are equally acceptable topics). With each question, we grow more invested in Nandita. We find ourselves rooting for her as she navigates this challenge both in the world and in herself.

It'd be impossible for us to do so if she merely danced around the issue. The refreshingly conversational tone here makes you feel as though Nandita were not only writing but also speaking to a close friend. To her, we're not scary professional admissions officers who'll decide her fate; we're simply peers, the recipients of a normal teenage girl's musings on life's struggles.

Craft

AS WITH MANY OTHER EXAMPLES, THIS piece begins with a bang. The dialogue is bluntly unexpected—a single line uttered by someone who isn't the author. Places of worship are known for their inclusivity, so many American readers, unused to the Indian religious context, immediately wonder what this girl could've possibly done to be cast away by her own mother. The result? An effective hook.

The author then follows this intriguing moment with a uniquely complex paragraph, which offers some context on the situation. Alternating between narration and internal monologue, it's almost a stream of consciousness, drawing the reader into Nandita's inner world. Now, we get to see how she feels, how she thinks, and how she processes her experiences. We're right there, stung by her embarrassment and wishing we could do something to help. Nonetheless, Nandita underlines this episode with tragicomic statements that humorously offset the gravity of the situation: "Could the week get any worse? Apparently, yes."

Not to disappoint after her rousing start, however, Nandita uses the full canvas of the narrative that follows. Every pointed word choice—such as "unobtrusively," "stammered," "constellation," or "snickered"—truly serves as a brushstroke to *paint the picture* of each scene.

EXERCISE

What truly angers you about society? Without lifting your pen/pencil, freewrite your frustration onto this page. Now, what would be the best channel to communicate this message to a broader audience?

Beyond Skin Deep: My Journey with Krishna's Dharma

SEERAT SINGH

Delhi-NCR

Columbia University

KRISHNA: THE DEFENDER OF DHARMA

My teeth chattered while I perused an illustrated account of Lord Vishnu's eighth incarnation. Refrigerated anesthesia and air-conditioning popped prickly goosebumps all over my skin. As I lay, back bare, waiting to be ushered into a new treatment room each week, Lord Krishna and his legend were my only constants.

Back in eighth grade, I paid weekly visits to Dr Kiran's Dermatology Clinic. Erasing the blue-black patches blemished across my arms, neck, and back meant that I wouldn't be an outlier anymore. My peers wouldn't scrutinize my complexion as they did when I emerged from the pool and skipped to the changing room...

"What happened to your neck?"

My friends huddled around me, pointing fingers. I felt like an installation on display, only no one seemed to appreciate what they saw. Teary-eyed, I trudged into the nearest shower stall, shuffling into my uniform and fixing a towel around my neck. Back home, I applied layers of sunscreen, desperate to block out the sun. I even started "forgetting" my swimsuit at home. The image of me trotting toward the ocean drifted from memory, replaced by the silhouette of a child longing to plunge into the water.

Before long, I lay atop the examination table at Dr Kiran's clinic—my new Saturday morning hangout. "Will the laser make any visible changes?" I questioned every week, prompting her to specify the intensity of the laser and how deeply it would penetrate my skin. Sensing my agitation, she patiently explained how the patches resulted from my amniotic sac being temporarily detached from my mother's placenta. She said this made me unique. For me, however, the unevenness of my skin represented my fear of being different, of being left out.

Anesthesia, Krishna, and finally the laser. Even after fifteen sittings, the treatment made little difference. It was supposed to be okay someday, but nobody knew when.

Was it worth spending the next n *Saturdays at Dr. Kiran's?*

What would Krishna, the defender of Dharma, do?

Krishna is portrayed in Hindu mythology as blue-skinned, yet he never perceived this as an obstacle on the path of Dharma. Whether he swirls with Radha or steers Arjuna's chariot, Krishna's dark skin tone is a mystical representation of cosmic grace and heroic bravery. The color symbolizes all-inclusiveness, a powerful metaphor for the vast expanse of the ocean and ideas stretching beyond human perception.

Going by the laws of Dharma, it was necessary to release oneself from the shackles of the mind. Just as I had been conditioned to be fearful, I had to train myself to be free. As Krishna says in 5:6 of the *Bhagavad Gita*: "Elevate yourself through the power of your mind, and do not degrade yourself, for the mind can be the friend and also the enemy of the self."

I had been viewing myself through the perspectives of others, not realizing that true beauty emanates from within. I once again visualized myself in the pool, fluttering my limbs like a butterfly's wings. It was time for me to break out of my cocoon, uplift myself, and soar over the seas, or rather in them. I ceased treatment and started swimming privately again. 15, 30, 45, and finally 60 minutes. I built my confidence, step by step. Three months later, I returned to the pool at school. The next time my friends asked, "What happened to your neck?" I dove into the scientific story of my birth.

While a lot has changed over the last four years, *Krishna: The Defender of Dharma* is still my only constant. As a PADI-certified diver, I carry my now-tattered book on each of my scuba diving adventures. Whether in the Maldives or the Andamans, Krishna's legend and the swirling shoals of fish remind me to embrace my imperfections and appreciate the beauty of diversity around me.

Summary

AHA, A COMMON LITTLE GENRE WE like to call the "Unusual Trait/Experience Essay." They stick in your mind because of their uniqueness; you can't help but remember them. AOs will thus apply the label of "Olympic gold medalist sprinter" or "World traveler of 100+ countries" or "18-year-old brain cancer survivor." Luckily, these are the kinds of narratives that basically write themselves. With Seerat, we had something notable in her skin condition. It made sense to harp on this since she was going to be in a basket with plenty of other Indian STEM women with less-interesting hooks to showcase. All her projects aligned with an engineering niche, which would certainly be discussed in her supplements. The CAE was an opportunity to present the human being whose scientific orientation perhaps shaped her interest in dermatology and Lord Krishna's blue skin. Even her swimming angle could be worked in. We just needed to get up close and personal. We needed to know the story.

Values

GROWING UP, EVERYONE HATES BEING DIFFERENT. For most, it's a relatively trivial matter that produces angst: height, weight, social awkwardness, and the like. Maybe it's something heftier, like poverty, dysfunctional family, or extreme physical deformity. Regardless, no one likes bitterness and pessimism—certainly not AOs. When you possess maturity like Seerat's, you develop wisdom. At no point does she demonize her peers; instead, she sympathizes with them. By the end, she even begins to teach them. Students like her will thrive in a diverse campus setting, where all sorts of backgrounds and perspectives coexist. It's Seerat's Intellectual Vitality that makes her so curiously human. It gives her warmth where others might appear cold.

How many kids her age are reading the *Bhagavad Gita* regularly? How many can quote it? We feel endeared by Seerat's pioneering spirit, how she channels the courage to finally reveal her true self without hiding. That's the kind of boldness AOs want to get behind. They want to feel inspired, not deflated!

Perspective

THE KRISHNA PARALLEL WORKS INCREDIBLY WELL to provide readers with context. So many authors approach these essays as though they were the first to ever experience problems! Seerat, on the other hand, seeks guidance from her own cultural roots, from others who've overcome similar hurdles. There's an appreciation for the *Bhagavad Gita*, one of India's most cherished ancient texts, that functions as more than just a hollow reference. Seerat's capacity to make connections between her life (that of a 21st-century female teen) and Krishna's (that of a mythological male deity) underscores how she thinks. She notes, in a line resonating with her overall water and biology theme, that "The color symbolizes all-inclusiveness, a powerful metaphor for the vast expanse of the ocean and ideas stretching beyond human perception." This is how you elevate an otherwise straightforward narrative. Seerat is "building cathedrals," not just "laying bricks."

Authenticity

RIGHT FROM THE START, ONE GETS the sense that Seerat is revisiting a painful experience. Her determination to share that experience reveals that she wants us to feel it with her. Students usually leave out the embarrassing details, but those are what make a story relatable! When she discusses how "erasing the blue-black patches blemished across my arms, neck, and back meant that I wouldn't be an outlier anymore," we can certainly identify with the longing to simply be normal. When she "skipped to the dressing room," we can all remember moments of trying to disappear. We also shudder during the scene when "...friends huddled around [her], pointing fingers." "I felt like an installation on display," she states, "only no one seemed to appreciate what they saw." A simple, effective metaphor that recalls the poet T.S. Eliot, who wrote of feeling like "a patient etherized upon a table." No one seeks to be dehumanized in this way. We get the admission of being "teary-eyed," especially poignant coming from a young woman in today's age of the #GirlBoss who must be "tough" and "collected" like her male counterparts.

Consequently, we care about Seerat as a character and as a person. We want to see her feel better. Only she doesn't present that narrative as we expect. After weighing the physical and emotional costs of these ongoing procedures, she decides they aren't worth it. She's reached her low point, with refreshing candor, and you can't help but think of her as a real person, not some Superwoman with no struggles. The paradox is that openness makes her stronger, not weaker.

Craft

A STRAIGHTFORWARD NARRATIVE, THIS ESSAY REQUIRED no fancy gimmicks or tricks. The author's personality was one of simplicity and warmth, so that's what she conveyed. Instead of focusing so much on form, we see her making use of detail as her primary literary device. The opening sentences really stage the scene, putting us right in her skin as she experiences this cold, clinical moment:

> My teeth chattered while I perused an illustrated account of Lord Vishnu's eighth incarnation. Refrigerated anesthesia and air-conditioning popped prickly goosebumps all over my skin. As I lay, back bare, waiting to be ushered into a new treatment room each week, Lord Krishna and his legend were my only constants.

As always, it's the details that really sell us. Throughout, Seerat employs concerted word choices in an attempt to make a visceral impression. We see the "goosebumps," the "patches," the "examination table." We feel the "agitation." The metaphor of "butterfly's wings" at the end captures an arresting image of how flying through air and darting through water can be one and the same. *Huh*. A science-oriented author with a penchant for scriptural study and rhetorical technique? Sounds interesting.

EXERCISE

Identify a time when you were misunderstood by others. What would you say to them now?

From Ghee to PCBs: Finding Art in Engineering and Cooking

VANSH MANTRI

Delhi-NCR

Carnegie Mellon University

MASHING THE BAATI WITH MY HANDS, relishing it with the sumptuous warmth and aroma of my Dadi's *arhar daal*, I wondered what made hers so special.

"It's *ghee*, beta." She chuckled.

"*Ghee?*" I frowned. How could something so simple and insignificant make the food taste so good?

"Yes. *Ghee*. I made it with my own hands."

Living by technologist Walter O'Brien's philosophy of utilitarianism, I never cultivated an appreciation for art, leaning instead towards mathematics and machines. I would even mock my sister's calligraphy, telling her how "useless" it was when she could just get the words printed faster and more accurately.

"You'll never understand this craft or appreciate the elegance in its flaws," she'd say, fuming at my ineptitude.

"Perhaps, but my Alex Brush script is so much better than whatever you're doing." My badgering would continue until she'd utter those five dreadful words—"Papa, Vansh is irritating me!" —and I'd flee like The Flash...

My initial encounter with a solder iron was at one of Faridabad's biggest electronic labs, where an assistant revealed to me the magic of this *kalakari*. As I learned to meld each little connection of a simple push-button circuit, a surprising beauty emerged that I couldn't have imagined.

At first, it was just joining wires. Later, however, I felt like a painter gently guiding my iron brush with just the right amount of tin paint at the right spot on my PCB canvas. Even as the pungent smoke from the burning metal filled my nostrils, I began to feel like someone different. Almost...like an *artist!*

Reflecting with the director of the lab, I regaled him with tales of my new discovery.

He laughed. "Nobody wants the hassle of soldering when they can easily get PCBs 3-D printed."

Somehow I felt offended. 'Why would anyone prefer the mundaneness of 3-D printing to this exquisite art?'

He replied with a smirk, "Well...because it's faster and more accurate."
How ironic.

I hated to admit it, but I finally understood my sister's love for calligraphy. Soldering resonated with me on a subatomic level. The simplicity in the process—peeling two wires, entangling them with each other, adding just a tiny amount of freshly melted solder wire, then a heat shrink tube to bind them forever—spoke to my essential nature: a Faridabad boy with a desire to innovate and a distaste for opulence. Emulating my grandmother's culinary artistry, I too wanted to build things *with my own hands.*

Months later, developing the first prototype of my own microcontroller board, I soldered every connection with utmost precision. I wanted to understand how individual components—transistors, resistors, relays—functioned in tandem with one another. Unifying disparate elements into a single whole unveiled the captivating nature of systems. Through first principles, I could now comprehend the unique application of each constituent, connecting it with others to produce something original.

I realized there is a certain finesse and satisfaction that emanates from the practice of creating from scratch. While *ghee* may just seem like cooked butter, by simmering it oneself, one can appreciate its purity, its essence, its relation to surrounding ingredients. The poise and novelty required to make things with my own hands forge a mystical connection between my creation and me. Like the atoms that compose all matter in the universe, it is the interplay of distinguishable elements, and the way they bond with each other, that makes anything whole. When simplified to its root, anything can be refashioned in our own image.

Simple is not just harder than complex; it is the basis for innovation. By breaking down an idea to its core, I uncover its potential for broader application. My distinct perspective enables me to visualize and dream in unanticipated ways. Applying this philosophy of reductionism in engineering and life has transformed me from a simple utilitarian to an artist with an iron brush.

Summary

OUR MAN(TRI) VANSH WAS THE FUN type of student that American universities love. An Indian male STEM applicant hailing from Delhi-NCR, he had few reliable hooks to his advantage, but he did have one thing going for him: the right kind of enthusiasm. What so often hinders kids in this basket is being too reserved and vocational. Vansh was quite the opposite. He also had a niche: electrical engineering instead of the standard computer science. His interests genuinely lay in building electronics, not software. Meanwhile, he loved the idea of simply learning and thinking. That, combined with a winning, self-aware charm, most certainly pushed him up and over other Standard Strong candidates. His CAE captures that difference beautifully.

Values

VANSH'S ESSAY IS ABOUT MANY THINGS—ART, technology, philosophy, tradition—but at its emotional core, it's about culture. This point is critical, since applicants from big satellite cities like Faridabad, just south of New Delhi, often struggle to identify elements of their heritage worth discussing. One of the best ways to succeed in that endeavor is to harness one's relationships with family. The "Family

Essay" or "Grandparent Essay" is a common trope nowadays, but if handled well, can deliver much heart. Here, our earnest Vansh wonders how his Dadi's *arhar daal* could be "so special." That genuine curiosity takes him on a journey to reconcile his interests not only with her but also with his sister (another trope, the "Sibling Essay"). As a result of how these discussions transpire, we feel that he possesses a warmth and appreciation for the people in his life; the essay reads human. For the Indian male STEM applicant in particular, it becomes critical to convey such intimacy. There's a sense that his cultural rootedness will impel him to revere others' cultures, too. He'll have something to contribute to a college campus.

And if family functions as the through line keeping the entire narrative grounded in authenticity, then it's Vansh's mental life that really charms us. As we've reiterated throughout this book, American universities deeply value the liberal arts mindset. It's cherished because it's so rare—especially among international applicants, who've typically been trained by a vocational education philosophy (*ratta*, as Indians bemoan). During the course of this 650-word piece, we glimpse interests in the culinary arts, manual labor, philosophy of technology, calligraphy, soldering, 3D printing, chemistry, and cosmology. It's all over the place, but in the best possible way! A reader might glean that this student would take advantage of all opportunities to learn widely as well as deeply on campus. He wouldn't be limited to a narrow pre-professional path. (Otherwise, he would've written an SOP focused exclusively on his wish to study electrical engineering.) You can indeed discuss your academic passions in a CAE, but if you do, please ensure that you add some of that liberal arts sparkle! It's no wonder that Carnegie Mellon—a school rooted in interdisciplinary thinking, especially between technology and the arts—resonated with this young man's Intellectual Vitality.

Perspective

DO YOU HAVE ANY DOUBT THAT the author of this piece is smart? Why or why not? From the very start, he's on a mission to answer an intellectual question: "How could something so simple and insignificant make the food taste so good?" Dadi's initial answer is only the beginning, however. By the end of the narrative, he discovers that her cooking, his sister's craft, and his own soldering interest all go...

hand in hand. Indeed, this image of working "with [one's] own hands" links every major discussion. There's another angle here: historically, Indian society has failed to hold manual labor in high regard; therefore, Vansh highlights another differentiating quality—the capacity to not only cogitate but also to roll up his sleeves and breathe life into his ideas. It gives Vansh the platform to offer an extended riff on a subject clearly close to his intellectual core.

For three whole paragraphs, he steps aside from "storytelling," per se, in favor of intense, meditative reflection. Having discovered that he has a touch of old-school within ("a distaste for opulence"), matched with "a desire to innovate," he begins to truly wrestle with what it takes to grasp how complex things work. Our enlightened author is now capable of systems thinking, a critical holistic skill in modern technology spaces. One must appreciate how each constituent of a whole can be combined "with others to produce something original." This ability to think in terms of "first principles," another critical holistic skill in all fields, reveals a mature young mind capable of real problem solving and innovation. He's even managed to brand himself: "from a simple utilitarian to an artist with an iron brush." How many kids his age have that level of self-awareness?

Authenticity

WHAT MAKES VANSH A WINNING PROTAGONIST here rests entirely on his openness and willingness to grow. The whole essay is just one big comeuppance, at the expense of our unwitting author. There's no malice or ill will, however. He admits early on that "I never cultivated an appreciation for art, leaning instead towards mathematics and machines," only to find later that there's an "irony" in his love for the old-fashioned *kalakari* of soldering. That little insight, played in deadpan, highlights how Vansh isn't afraid to be real with his readers. He's a relatable figure: a willful Philistine, an annoying younger brother, a strict traditionalist. He gets better with time, as the best of us do. Most kids want to present themselves in a perfect light, but how insipid is that? We support Vansh all the more because he's clearly *not* that kid. Keeping things so personal and jovial during the first two thirds of the essay helps make the more pretentious discussion at the end more palatable and justified. We see it as a part of his character arc, the conclusion of his natural path.

Craft

OF COURSE, FOR ALL HIS (NEWFOUND) love of art, Vansh was no wordsmith in the most literary sense. Instead, he dealt in ideas. Intellectual subjects got him going, so we had him insert allusions and references to his favorite thinkers, like Walter O'Brien. Getting specific with "utilitarianism" or "reductionism" makes Vansh appear as a serious, knowledgeable student, not the kind who's only skimmed the contents of his philosophy syllabus. But most importantly—as with so many authors—the devil's in the details all around. We can emote and connect in the opening because Vansh delivers such visceral descriptions of his dadi's cooking practices. Our senses are stimulated by language choices like "the sumptuous warmth and aroma" or "the pungent smoke from the burning metal filled my nostrils." He truly sells us on what makes soldering, which might appear dry or boring to a non-electrical engineer, riveting. He writes with such descriptive enthusiasm and love that it's impossible not to see the world through his eyes. This is how admissions officers, most of whom are non-specialists in the fields of their applicants, wish to feel. So, make your passion palpable!

EXERCISE

Have you developed a newfound appreciation for something you once hated or dismissed? What was that experience like? How did you come to see things differently?

BEYOND SILENCE: FINDING STRENGTH IN LISTENING

AVIJAN CHANDHOK

Jaipur

Carnegie Mellon University

ALL EARS

I have been told not to talk about this for as long as I can remember.
"...This will put you in a different light."
"No one will look at you the same..."
And so, as a child, I agreed.

During school bus rides, while everyone traded gossip and listened to music on their headphones, I refrained—remembering my doctor's warnings. But just to fit in and appear *normal*, I would still plug mine in without any music playing. I had to—such high decibels could be fatal for my hearing.

The only ones privy to this secret were my parents, who desperately sought to maintain a façade of perfection. They believed that if we didn't talk about it, it would disappear.

My life was the show 24, every hour bringing a new problem. In front of my friends, I had to don my mask of normalcy. At school, I struggled to keep up when several people spoke at once. Listening tests were always difficult. At home, the scenario was always the same: my mother screaming at my father to give up his alcohol and cigarettes. While he remained unaffected, my baby sister cried in the corner.

Every hour, every minute, every second of my life was an ongoing battle—I was ready to surrender.

However, inspiration came in the form of an unlikely source. My summer school instructor, Duha, was afflicted with the same condition: unilateral hearing loss, or total deafness in one ear. I marveled at her confidence as she disclosed the details of her disability at the introductory session. Her candid admission revealed to me that my hearing problem could be an ally, not an adversary.

I was not "perfect," but my imperfections—paradoxically—made me whole. My adversity became my greatest strength. The limited supply of my hearing drove an exponential increase in the demand for my listening, thus unveiling its true potential.

I had always been a good student. Now more than ever, I clung to my teachers' every word. I valued every phrase, every lesson, while my peers remained casual—leaning back, disinterested, taking our teachings for granted. People assumed that hearing and listening were synonymous, but differentiating between them allowed me to realize the latter's true value. I may not possess the ability to hear to the fullest, but I could still value what I had. By providing a safe space for my friends, one where they could vent and share, I could help them shed their own façades of perfection.

Conditions at home also demanded that I step up and serve as a pillar of support. Dealing with my father's stubbornness and my mother's breakdowns—all while ensuring my baby sister remained unaffected—was a herculean task. I needed to put my newfound superpower to practice.

"Avi, I didn't want to be the person I am today. I want to change, but I'm trapped by my addictions."

Listening to my father discuss his issues in a safe space forged—for the first time—a bond of empathy. Finally, he was free to reveal what he truly felt, thus allowing me to approach the problem differently. From blaming him, telling him to "be better," I began affirming him. My father never wanted to disrupt the household; he was imprisoned by his debts, and the compulsions they fostered. Through our newfound dialogue, we established a mutual respect, and he even welcomed professional help.

Be it with my family, peers, or teachers, I have honed my appreciation of others over time. As the challenges in my life grow more strenuous,

I refine my ability to listen, to empathize, to investigate the depths of any problems they face. Their secrets are safe with me.

Today, the necessity of listening and empathizing has never been greater, and thus to ensure that I never abandon this virtue, I will always have an ear to lend.

Summary

WE DISCUSS AT LEAST ONE OTHER applicant in this list as a superhero, but Avijan truly embodied the role. A student at a highly reputed North-Indian school, he certainly possessed privileges—but also disadvantages. Immediately, his significant hearing impairment jumped out as something we must showcase. "Diversity," of course, is the great buzzword at American universities these days, and it goes far beyond race/ethnicity, gender/sexual identity, religion, or political affiliation. One's ability status can offer perspectives that other traits cannot. Avijan thus had a minor hook, which he was certainly going to need as a Standard Strong economics/finance/business kid—a dime a dozen within his demographic—with no extremely notable achievements. His best bet was to amplify what made him so inspiring to us all: his overwhelming positivity. People may like to criticize Superman these days, but there's a reason he remains such a touchstone of popular culture, even for non-Americans. We look to wholesome heroes to be reminded of what we can be.

Values

IF YOU HAD TO SAY WHAT strikes you about this essay, it'd probably be its maturity. The author reads as someone well beyond his years, yet not in a pretentious way. It's bold and courageous to discuss something so difficult for him, no doubt, but one never gets the sense that he's trying to exploit it. This is merely the author's story, one he desperately needs to tell. While covering such topics, most students stumble and fall into navel-gazing and negativity. Avijan avoids all that by keeping his focus simultaneously inward and outward. He clearly has an altruistic, do-gooder attitude, displaying concern and action for his distraught mother and vulnerable sister. He strives to provide a "safe space" for his friends. And perhaps most notably, he maintains compassion for his struggling father. Now, in forward-thinking healthcare circles, the term "addiction" is increasingly being discouraged in favor of "substance abuse disorder," while "addict" is considered demonizing. It thus speaks volumes about Avijan's character that he aligns with this burgeoning trend by being so tolerant and understanding. His kindness and patience reflect someone with gravitas, even wisdom. There's no malice or bitterness. You can imagine him being a similarly positive influence in his future campus community. Just imagine how the essay would read had he chosen to linger solely on the negative emotions of the opening paragraphs!

Perspective

WHEN YOU PICTURE AN ESSAY THAT fits into the "Unusual Trait/ Experience" and "Disability Essay" genres, like this one, you expect a standard discussion of how the author is different. For example, they may mention how they're disabled but actually possess plenty of autonomy. But Avijan isn't your standard kid. Like any great superhero, he learns to turn his weakness into a superpower. "I was not 'perfect', but my imperfections—paradoxically—made me whole." Such a statement avoids the obvious by claiming that the author here is actually a fuller human being thanks to his perceived deficiencies. The lack of typical ability drives him to listen more than the average person—a point that highlights the subtle semantic difference between "hearing" and "listening."

And this idea extends beyond his immediate context. Avijan is perceptive enough to recognize that "the necessity of listening and empathizing has never been greater" in today's society. He's got the macro view—something so many applicants lack—but also an acute concern for the micro. As much as this superhero wants to help the world at large, he's just as attuned to the needs of his own family. That one pivotal paragraph with his father constitutes the heart of the essay: he's a compassionate, understanding, precocious individual who doesn't judge. How many students his age could handle such a fraught situation with genuine curiosity and affirmation? How many could acknowledge that "My father never wanted to disrupt the household; he was imprisoned by his debts, and the compulsions they fostered?" These are developments that reflect higher-order reasoning and emotional maturity—states that even many so-called "adults" never reach.

Authenticity

THE BEST ESSAYS HOOK US WITH vulnerability right from the very beginning. They draw us in, like a tractor beam, and never let go until the end. Thus, when our author writes, "I have been told not to talk about this for as long as I can remember," we're immediately invested. We want to know what the mysterious pronoun "this" is referring to. Our minds begin racing, as the narrator is clearly inviting us into their private life. We feel entrusted with their secret. It's as through we're their confidant, and the following confession is for us and us alone. In the following paragraphs, Avijan details what life's like as a young man with a disability. Each point reads less like a sensationalist episode or an angry rant and more like a simple instance of unburdening oneself to a friend.

Anyone can relate to Avijan's shame-ridden upbringing, his attempt to appear "normal." One doesn't need a disability to grasp his predicament. Even when he delves into the dysfunctional aspects of his family, with great honesty and courage, we feel his wish to "surrender." Such words aren't what we typically associate with the image of a Superman—a perfect, ideal being among the gods who presumably flies from strength to shining strength. Avijan here is willfully raw and unfiltered. He's believable. So many applicants miss this point: being a superhero isn't just about having power. Their weakness to Kryptonite merely makes them human—and their achievements all the more meaningful.

Craft

ONE THING WE LOVED ABOUT AVIJAN was that he simply had the right attitude. There was no nastiness or spite in our discussions. He was positive, yes, but he was also fun. Applicants never have enough of that! Who wants to read about bland, chipper role models all day? Avijan took a liking to playfulness with language, and it shows. Seemingly throwaway lines like "The limited supply of my hearing drove an exponential increase in the demand for my listening, thus unveiling its true potential" prove crucial, for they say more about the student than what meets the *ear*. Wordplay is a critically underused technique for demonstrating cleverness; it also keeps the reading experience engaging. Many a standard essay marked by tropes—conflict with parents, overcoming an obstacle, experiencing an epiphany after consulting some authority figure—can be elevated by just demonstrating joy in the writing. Why not have a final punchline riffing on the idiom, "to lend an ear?" Why not include a title, riffing on another related idiom, being "all ears?" That levity and attention to detail keeps the essay grounded as well as memorable. Oh, and his major was actually in the domain of economics, finance, and business. Subtle puns for the win!

EXERCISE

What's your secret superpower? In other words, what's some talent or skill you possess that helps improve your life and others'? Why is it important, and how have you honed it over time?

From the Ganges to Bali: Searching for the Divine Within

TARISHI BHUTANI

Delhi-NCR

Stanford University

240 MILLION PEOPLE. THE LARGEST GATHERING in human history. *The Maha Kumbh Mela.*

In the town of Prayagraj, I stood just meters from the holy confluence of the Ganges, Yamuna, and mythical Saraswati rivers. Raised in a Hindu family, I had heard ancient miraculous tales about *Kumbh*: those who performed the sacred immersion would receive the blessings of *amrit*, the elixir of immortality. Bristling with anticipation, I did not feel the whip of the chilly wind.

Finally, it was my turn. As I proceeded to take the dip, the holy aura of the water was superseded by a stinging sensation in my eyes. The murky shallows were rife with plastic bags and other debris. And there was the stench from rotting organic material floating on the surface.

As I re-emerged from the water, I was baffled by the irony. And that bafflement soon became disillusionment. As I pulled myself onto the bank and shuffled back to our tent, I could not help but recall a previous diving experience.

I remembered the moment I heaved my oxygen tank and fastened my flippers. I stood at the edge of the boat, my heart thumping, itching to leap into the boundless blue ocean. Illumined by arrows of sunlight, I witnessed mountains of coral reefs beneath me. There were species, food chains, entire ecosystems beneath the surface, I had never appreciated. And as I reveled in the dances performed by schools of fish, I was flooded with a new sense of humility. I was humbled to behold the diversity of my planet's inhabitants, and how little I knew about them. That day, the waters of Tulamben, Bali rejuvenated me. Every part of my being was in harmony—the physical, the intellectual, the emotional...even the spiritual.

Why did the *Kumbh* dive not invoke similar emotions? Why did it not revitalize me? In fact, on the contrary, it compelled me to cast aspersions on my own religious identity. Why did I not feel a deeper connection with the holy waters of the Ganges, as did the countless other devotees surrounding me? Was I not a Hindu? Or worse, was I a *bad* Hindu?

Amidst 240 million people, I suddenly felt alone.

I scanned the crowd scattered along the *ghats*, spotting an old woman in a saffron cotton sari. Despite her limp, she cast herself into the water to conduct her ablutions. But although she emerged shivering, there was a sparkle in her eye and a smile tugging at the corners of her mouth. She had undoubtedly experienced a mystical connection.

Not unlike my experience in Bali.

Two incidents, with essentially the same stimulus, invoked contrasting feelings within me. But could there be an unlikely union?

As I pondered the strange parallels, I was reminded of a couplet by the mystic Sufi poet Kabir:

"The musk is embedded in the navel, yet the deer looks for the fragrance in the forest.

In the same way, God is present in everyone's heart, but no one notices him."

Kabir's philosophy states that God resides within every soul, and while humans seek him in external manifestations, they remain unaware that the essence of the divine lies within them. Everyone is seeking a connection to something larger than themselves—a belief, a value, an ideal. A purpose.

And at that moment, enveloped by the swirling pandemonium of the *ghats,* a new realization dawned on me: people are diverse entities free to mystify or *demystify* their experiences. There are many paths, and every seeker can find the one that resonates with their core. For some, it is theoretical physics. For others, *Kumbh*. For me, it was the Balinese coral reefs. Each is a quest for an expanded sense of self.

As I walked away from the expectations associated with the *Maha Kumbh Mela*, I submerged my conflict in those very murky waters of the Ganges and found solace in the sea of devotees.

Summary

YOU KNOW WHAT IT'S LIKE WHEN you encounter someone who's just different? That's how we felt getting to know Tarishi. Right off the bat, her interest in psychology caught our attention. Increasingly, Indian women have been turning to this subject for their major (since it's often considered STEM for employment visa purposes), but at the time, Tarishi's choice made her something of a trendsetter. Still, it was her niche within that space that really got us going. Unlike her counterparts, she was interdisciplinary. She was quirky. No one could put her into a box. Such personalities align perfectly with the American vibe—particularly that of the quirkiest elite university, Stanford. To gain admission, Tarishi needed to upend readers' expectations of a so-called Indian "soft science" applicant (just as her own expectations were upended during a fateful riverside event). You could say she blew it out of the water.

Values

TALK ABOUT ANTI-STEREOTYPING. THIS CEREBRAL ESSAY has Intellectual Vitality written all over it. Seriously, what's it even about? Ostensibly religion, sure, but there's also a scoop of Indian poetry tossed in, a mention of "theoretical physics"—even an extended riff on marine biology. Elite universities love to see such rampant curiosity delivered with academic depth. They don't want to read about yet another kid who's simply memorized the bare minimum to get through their course. Such students rarely retain what they learn, and they certainly don't write with such scholarly vigor.

Your first thought might've been a different university value, however. Indeed, there's exceptional courage on display here. After all, it's bold to resist that temptation to swim with the current; with Tarishi, you feel that such a thought never even crossed her mind. Challenging religion is decidedly not safe (picture Nani or Dadi reading this!), but it's a worthy, welcome subject matter. Clearly, the problem is important to the author, which is what the personal essay genre is all about. And in case you were worried, Tarishi remains simultaneously "culturally rooted" and respectful throughout. Her interest in the more esoteric elements of her Hindu heritage (*amrit* and Kabir instead of the more commonly known *Bhagavad Gita* or Gandhi) confirms that she takes her background quite seriously. She's never dismissive—"There are many paths, and every seeker can find the one that resonates with their core"—but rather understanding. It's the kind of sophistication American universities seek; thus, Tarishi will undoubtedly thrive in a diverse campus community, where differing traditions intermingle like the rivers at Prayagraj.

Perspective

AGAIN, TARISHI IS A QUINTESSENTIAL THINKER: she observes, ponders, questions. This fact makes it easy to identify insight—the whole essay is insightful! At its core, this story is about the juxtaposition of seeming opposites: self vs. other, India vs. Bali, right vs. wrong. Tarishi's great research question, if you will, is encapsulated in the dichotomy she highlights about midway through: "Two incidents, with essentially the same stimulus, invoked contrasting feelings within me. But could there be an unlikely union?" Like any good scientist, she assesses her initial hypothesis and arrives at a new thesis, even a new theory. Maybe, she finds, there's a different way of seeing things.

Additionally, Tarishi is a meticulous kind of scientist. She documents the pilgrims' responses to the water and how they contrast with her own. Then, she offers her thoughts on gaining "humility" from the underwater "species, food chains, entire ecosystems." This immersion places her individual experience in a broader context of other organisms who must coexist. Few students are so in tune with themselves on the "physical, the intellectual, the emotional...even the spiritual" levels. They remain, instead, stuck within the bubbles of their immediate surroundings. The result is a transcendent quality encapsulated by Tarishi's ultimate takeaway: "Everyone is seeking a connection to something larger than themselves—a belief, a value, an ideal. A purpose." It's a high-minded, not-quite-religious, not-quite-secular idea. By resisting any neat, tidy conclusion either for or against faith, Tarishi presents herself as an intellectual with promising nuance.

Authenticity

WE'RE SURE YOU'LL AGREE: THIS ESSAY feels real. It's not just the topic or the technique, but rather the whole that's greater than the sum of its parts. From start to finish, Tarishi is being honest with us and with herself. She's unafraid to admit that the famed *Maha Kumbh Mela* is…a letdown. Most applicants fear being direct in this way, partly because their cultures have warned against revealing too much. The collectivism of India and other Eastern societies often trains students to avoid expressing their actual thoughts. One must simply accept things as they are and always have been, for Eastern societies are old civilizations with many ancient customs more or less set in stone. America, by contrast, is a new civilization. It's hardly two centuries young, and its entire founding is based on the romantic idea of "Independence" and freedom (of speech, religion, etc.). Therefore, when an Indian student like Tarishi speaks their language, elite universities' ears perk up.

Like a journalist, Tarishi unflinchingly records how the "The murky shallows were rife with plastic bags and other debris. And there was the stench from rotting organic material floating on the surface." In the pursuit of truthfulness, she refuses to paint her national home in purely positive terms. Many readers from her background can certainly identify with her sentiment. Particularly when she acknowledges that "As I re-emerged from the water, I was baffled by the irony," we see someone brave enough to address the elephant in the room. That boldness also manifests when she openly wonders, "Was I not a Hindu? Or worse, was I a bad Hindu?" Anyone who's been raised as a believer will likely find a similar question rise to the surface of their thoughts at some point in life. Its inevitable follow-up comes in the next sentence, a devastating single-line paragraph: "Amidst 240 million people, I suddenly felt alone." For an essay about human connection, Tarishi had to give us a stirring sense of its opposite.

Craft

IT'D BE FAIR TO SAY THAT this is a fairly accessible narrative (albeit with a flashback in the middle). That simplicity gives us a vast, open ocean to gain—ahem—depth. At their best, slice of life essays capture a single moment in time, drawing us into the finite episode as though we were truly there with the author.

See how Tarishi artfully hypes up the big event in the essay's stark opening line—"240 million people. The largest gathering in human history. *The Maha Kumbh Mela*"—only to deflate it soon after with visceral depictions of an unpleasant sensory experience. You turn your nose at the foul odor; you rub your eyes at the burning sensation. And then, you marvel at the contrast with the beautiful description of her Bali experience: "Illumined by arrows of sunlight, I witnessed mountains of coral reefs beneath me." Even so, it's how Tarishi circles back to the opening that really showcases her observational acumen. "But although she emerged shivering," she writes of the elderly pilgrim, "there was a sparkle in her eye and a smile tugging at the corners of her mouth." Such thoughtful descriptions, using unusual personification, make Tarishi the kind of detail-oriented scholar that colleges are dying to meet.

EXERCISE:

List 1–3 popular views that you disagree on. If you had ten minutes and the audience of the entire world, how would you present your case?

AGAINST THE TIDE: A SWIMMER'S JOURNEY TO SELF-DISCOVERY

GAURVI SINGHVI

Jaipur

Stanford University

02:53:46

The chill in the air hung heavy amidst the engulfing darkness. As I clambered up the rocky beach, my foot slipped on a patch of algae and I winced in pain. The bellow of the horn pierced the rhythmic thrum of the waves crashing against the shore.

There was no stepping back now. Before I knew it, I had dived into the deep, unknown ocean before me: the "Everest" of open-water swims. Water swirled around my limbs, embracing me in a familiar belonging. The confines of the pool had often made me feel like a fish in a glass bowl, but here in the limitless ocean, I felt free.

The sky grew brighter. With each stroke, my face was bathed in glorious sunshine, a stark contrast from the darkness into which I had plunged. Gulping saline water and energy drinks, I felt my stomach lurch and started vomiting. Still, I pressed onward—ankle throbbing, muscles screaming, the sharp stings of jellyfish burning my thigh.

My thoughts were my only company. One moment I was singing "Believer" in my head; the next, I was thinking of all the world's cities I wanted to visit. I thought of everything. I thought of nothing. Words ebbed like waves against my brain.

Eventually, when my mind ran out of distractions, I found myself face-to-face with the questions I had submerged for years. My demons, like sirens, were as real as the chafing on my skin and the sea lions prancing alongside me. Alluring voices murmured—*is all this torment worth it? For whom do you swim? You? Or perhaps the parents who have poured so much time and energy into your training?* I pictured my friends freely sleeping in, eating pizza, and asked, *"Had swimming taken more than it had given?"*

WHEN I ARRIVED AT FATEHSAGAR LAKE in Udaipur for the adult one-kilometer race, my coach looked down at my tiny twelve-year-old frame and said, "You can participate, but you won't get the prize money." No one expected me to finish, much less win. Their doubt in my potential drove me to stroke harder, kick faster, be better. I had to show them what a *little girl* could do. Show myself. If I could place second among 200 adult male swimmers, clearly I was stronger than I thought.

Years later, the same applied. My real battle wasn't against the tides in the ocean or the winds in the sky, but against my own mental drag. I had to be the girl I was at the Lake, motivated from within, not from without. The question was simple: *What did I want?*

Seeing the strife in my eyes as he followed alongside, my mentor Nick reminded me, "Darling, you're swimming the English Channel. Of course, it's going to hurt." My sail swiveled and I caught my second wind. I knew my body would carry on long as my mind did. These final few hours, I needed to fight for what I had always sought: transcendence. Nothing else mattered.

Slowly, I felt a renewed vigor in my strokes. Only now, the tide had turned. The harder I swam, the further out I was carried by the surge of the sea. The rocky coast grew hazier by the minute. Nevertheless, I was determined to conquer Everest. There were truths yet to prove. Potential was merely hypothesis, theory; there had to be *evidence* for belief. The belief in self.

16:21:30

The French waters gradually warmed as I clung to a jagged rock, anchoring myself to the foot of Cap Gris-Nez. The horn sounded yet again, and I hoisted the Indian tricolor with tears filling my goggles.

At that moment, I was finally free. Free of expectation, of constraint, of doubt. By immersing myself in the briny waters of my psyche, I became one with my purpose. I became one with myself.

That alone made my torment worthwhile.

Summary

SO, REMEMBER HOW WE SAID THAT there's no such thing as the one perfect essay for any particular applicant? That there may be many potential options for The Essay Only You Can Write? Yeah, we lied. In some extremely uncommon instances, there really is just one essay that makes sense. That's why the Common App offers its first prompt, which we like to call "How I'm Special." If you've done something truly extraordinary, like performing at Carnegie Hall, or have come from a truly extraordinary context, like being raised in a cult, then you should probably talk about that—not your average experience of struggling as the leader of your school's tech club.

Gaurvi had one of those rare, enviable situations of possessing a stellar, genuinely interesting profile with significant public recognition: an Indian woman from a highly reputed school in Rajasthan with a notable swimming + public speaking + politics interest. She was the youngest woman (Indian or not) to swim across the English Channel, for goodness' sake! Now, Gaurvi tried outlining a few ideas on other subjects, but we stopped her right there; this was the story! (Stanford certainly noticed, for they mentioned it in her acceptance letter as well as in the dean's welcome address during her freshman orientation.) Even better, Gaurvi was a strong writer, too. Fitting into the "Eternal" archetype, she had a gift for gripping, aesthetic prose. Some essays just write themselves...

Values

IF THERE'S ONE THING THAT GRABS you about Gaurvi's essay, it's her unrelenting ambition. Sure, she struggles along her fateful swim, but ultimately, she achieves her worthy goal. That's what you call tenacity, the sticktoitiveness to get the job done. You can picture someone who's overcome such torment certainly having no trouble making it through Stanford! "How you do anything is how you do everything," goes the saying. AOs are constantly seeking to extrapolate your potential from how you manage obstacles. These situations reveal character. It's not masochistic to feature a Pivot like this: "Nick reminded me, 'Darling, you're swimming the English Channel. Of, course it's going to hurt.'" In embracing resistance, Gaurvi demonstrates the mental toughness necessary to succeed across other domains as well.

Now, of course, most Sports Essays will attempt to showcase this sort of trait. What distinguishes Gaurvi's is her motivation to represent something bigger than herself. "Transcendence" is what she seeks. It's something both individualistic (a personal goal, in line with Western ideals) and collectivistic (a goal tied to her identity as a woman, formerly "a little girl.") You can see the subtle hints of feminism that feature more prominently in other aspects of her profile. Additionally, the brief allusions to "sirens" (Greek mythology) and existential ideas highlight a certain Intellectual Vitality that elevates the essay beyond readers' expectations.

Perspective

CERTAIN ESSAYS STUN US WITH THE depth of their complexity. Such power becomes all the more apparent when the subject and structure of the narrative is simple, as with Gaurvi's. On the surface, you have a run-of-the-mill Sports Essay (albeit one about an extraordinary experience!), but when you dive in, you find a vast sea of thoughts swimming in its murky deep. The anchor is Gaurvi's self-awareness. Unlike many champion achievers, she's just as much a thinker as she is an athlete. She constantly reveals how her mind works. Observations abound, such as her contrast between feeling confined like a "fish in a glass bowl" while at the pool and feeling free in the "limitless ocean." Later passages impel us to ask, who else would be reflecting on her life's purpose while tackling such a Herculean task?

Gaurvi contemplates her motivations, her parents' motivations, and even those of her friends. She places herself within a context, inviting us to ponder the virtues of teen sports, and more philosophically, the very nature of ambition itself. "There were truths yet to prove," she writes.

"Potential was merely a hypothesis, theory; there had to be evidence for belief. The belief in self." With each draft, we pushed Gaurvi to truly interrogate her journey because we knew her uncommon drive deserved due attention. In the final version, she makes the distinction between knowing what one is capable of and actually confirming it. It's a lesson many have yet to learn.

Authenticity

A COMMON STEREOTYPE OF ATHLETIC ACHIEVERS is that they don't feel like real people. They rise every morning at ungodly hours, maintain draconian diets, train all day long, and somehow still manage to get their schoolwork done. #Goals. These supermen and superwomen might be great sources of inspiration, but hardly the kind of folks we actually want to know. Luckily, Gaurvi displayed far more nuance than the peers in her basket. When we read her piece, we're intrigued by its consistent through line: her fraught relationship with ambition, with her parents...and with herself.

Truly, we can't reiterate how fortunate we are when we encounter a student who's actually happy to discuss their inner world. You can't just be a bland, impenetrable Hero or Heroine; you need to have an edge, some bite. You need to wear your heart on your (swimsuit) sleeve. Where does Gaurvi do this? Well, she starts off by sharing her difficulties. This is no picture-perfect #GirlBoss. We get "ankle throbbing, muscles screaming, the sharp stings of jellyfish burning my thigh." Okay, pretty normal confessions, right? But we also get "my stomach lurch" and "vomiting." These visceral descriptions really serve to make us feel what she feels, in that very moment. Most authors would sanitize such passages, but then, the authenticity would be lost.

Similarly, by acknowledging that she has "demons," Gaurvi welcomes a darker self-portrait than what might be expected of her. With great courage, she confronts the problem of autonomy and agency that so often plagues athletes like herself: "For whom do you swim? You? Or perhaps the parents who have poured so much time and energy into your training?" One can imagine most students in her situation wishing to express this sentiment, but feeling too afraid to say it aloud. Gaurvi respects her family's sacrifice, yet she's also human. She has needs and desires of her own—such as the wish to be like her friends, who get to eat pizza and sleep in. But we never see Gaurvi as a whiner or a complainer, which is a testament to her character. We simply see her as a fallible protagonist whom we inevitably cheer on. Everyone's susceptible to the monster called Envy; Gaurvi is simply willing to look him in his green eyes.

Craft

AGAIN, THIS IS A RELATIVELY STRAIGHTFORWARD story. What makes it interesting, beyond the values showcased, are the eloquent prose and curious structure. Marked by a preference for belabored language, Gaurvi is a highly descriptive writer. Her affinity for setting really brings you into the scene, in an almost cinematic manner. From the first few sentences, it's clear that the speaker's experience will be immersive. She melts into the landscape as "water swirled around my limbs, embracing me in a familiar belonging." When the scene shifts to a flashback, we see her as a child, standing up with confidence against her doubting male counterparts. The central image of "Everest" helps remind the reader that she's not simply crossing a lake here, though. This is a BIG DEAL, the sea-based equivalent of what many mountaineers strive for and fail at every single year—sometimes with deadly results.

And obviously, there's Gaurvi's quirky use of timestamps for each section. So much more than a cheap gimmick, they serve to mimic the feel of a stopwatch, a device swimmers will be all too familiar with. As we always say, it's one thing to include a cool innovation in form, but it's another to choose one that's meaningful. The posted times provide a level of realism; referring to something about space or plants or robots would've been pointless. Take it from the mastery you see here: impactful writing is all about the DETAILS.

EXERCISE

List 1–3 actions that are easy for you today but were difficult in the past. How did you push through those difficult moments to become who you are today? How can you continue to adopt a "growth mindset" to overcome present challenges?

LITERARY JOURNEYS AND TECHNOLOGICAL BRIDGES: CRAFTING A MODERN BABEL

ADITYA MEHTA

Mumbai

California Institute of Technology (Caltech)

I ENCOUNTERED THE TALE OF BABEL through chance.

Exploring the code behind the infinite *Library of Babel*, a digital repository of universal human knowledge, I was equally captivated by the Hebrew myth behind it: humankind, in a moment of hubris, strives to build a tower to heaven. To me, the parable revealed a profound truth. When we cannot communicate and share stories, when language is "confused," "so one does not understand the speech of the other"— the tower of life is doomed to crumble.

I keep my favorite stories on a neat shelf, carefully wrapped in cotton sheets (I can't afford the pages yellowing). My collection is neither fancy (save some first-edition *Hardy Boys*) nor as extensive as the *Library of Babel*. However, conversing with different authors has led me on far-away journeys through space and time, philosophical epiphanies, and friendships with unexpected characters.

Living in metropolitan Mumbai, nine-year-old me came to envy India's rural heartland through Ruskin Bond's fiction. In his quaint hill-stations, banyan trees towered over colorful markets, and farm animals became family members. On annual visits to my grandparents' home in rural Haryana, I delighted in the aroma of mustard buds, and chatted for hours with local farmers, amazed by their knowledge of every soil type. Just like Bond's characters. But returning from those trips, I would read reports of farmer suicides due to poor harvests. I felt unsettled.

At 12, my bucolic fantasies were overrun by *Brave New World*. Its artificially-engineered population hooked on happiness-inducing "soma" prompted me to question my growing technophilia. Previously enchanted by computers that could outsmart chess grandmasters, drive cars, and even "write" stories, I now began to view technology as a power capable of creating and destroying. While authors like Huxley and Atwood warned against the unfettered use of technology, Tolkien's eccentric wizard countered my growing pessimism. "There are other forces at work in this world," Gandalf told a disillusioned Frodo, "besides that of evil." Beyond turning unsuspecting children into lifelong nerds destined to heated online debates on why the Fellowship couldn't just "fly the eagles to Mordor," *Lord of the Rings* emphasized the necessity of virtuous action when faced with insurmountable darkness.

If four naïve hobbits from the Shire could save Middle-Earth, I too could dive headlong into the world's problems and be a changemaker.

Last year, while reading Delia Owens' *Where The Crawdads Sing*, the protagonist Kya offered a path to enact change. In Kya, I saw the farmers from my grandparents' village. Although ostracized and lacking formal education, she developed an impressive grasp of the Louisiana marsh in which she lived. Learning to write empowered her to share these insights. As I had witnessed first-hand, Indian farmers too possess an intergenerational knowledge of the fields in which they toil. However, as if afflicted by Babel's curse, successful practices of a particular community remain within its linguistic borders, failing to pollinate other regions.

Inspired by the Tower's myth (though maybe taking the wrong lesson), I leveraged my knowledge of natural language processing to build a platform for farmers to communicate, share resources, and learn online, transcending divisions of regional language.

Khetibaat: agricultural conversations.

Working closely with farmers, agricultural professors, and NGOs, I developed features to "unconfuse" communication across 12 Indian vernaculars: WhatsApp chatbots, integration with government resources, and text-to-speech feed a growing platform that connects over 200 farmers, across six villages in four Indian states. Through *Khetibaat*, I'm expanding my bookshelf, making it accessible to millions of farmers, an agricultural *Library of Babel*.

However, this endeavor is only the prologue.

As I continue to fill the chapters of my bildungsroman, I'll constantly converse with the great minds behind books, seeking comfort, inspiration, and enlightenment. I hope that human beings will someday understand one another perfectly enough to build together without hubris, or, at least, eradicate the farming crisis.

Summary

WE'RE ALWAYS WARY OF TROPES. THE Do-Gooder wishing to eradicate poverty. The MUNer wishing to design policies for a peaceful world. And of course, the Indian Male STEM Applicant.

Aditya was one such student—and aiming for computer science, no less! Had he simply discussed his passion for coding in this essay, it would've been predictable. Trite. But Aditya took the infamous "What Fascinates Me" prompt in another direction, highlighting his inspirations from literary works and how they shaped his thinking around his primary project. It wasn't a typical Project/Activity Essay; the initiative served more as a culmination of his intellectual journey. The achievement he makes so neatly ties together the lessons he garnered from the vast array of books he digested. We therefore appreciate not just Aditya's technical prowess, but also his maturity. The rest is history. Or rather, mythology.

Values

FROM THE VERY BEGINNING, WE AS readers have no doubt that Aditya is a seeker of wisdom. How many teenagers are intent on discovering or creating "a digital repository of universal human knowledge?" But this isn't an isolated statement. We see Aditya's reverence for *gyaan* through his treatment of the classics on his shelves, each of which is meticulously wrapped in cotton sheets to prevent the pages from yellowing. Only a true book lover would invest the time in such a practice! And if this is how he regards his collection, the AO will naturally surmise that he'll respect all the intellectual resources available at an esteemed institution like Caltech.

However, Aditya balances aspiration with the contrasting value of humility. He understands that to achieve lofty heights, one must be rooted equally deep into the ground. Without this modesty, our towers to heaven are doomed to crumble. Thankfully, Aditya isn't content with simply imbibing lessons from ancient scriptures. He ponders the deeper reasons behind the tower's downfall, extracting insights that he later applies while building his own miniature Babel: *Khetibaat*.

With every turn of the page, Aditya is inculcating and reinforcing more principles that help him navigate life's challenges. His distillation of *The Lord of the Rings* trilogy is especially touching, revealing the deeper motivations behind his endeavors:

> Lord of the Rings emphasized the necessity of virtuous action when faced with insurmountable darkness. If four naïve hobbits from the Shire could save Middle-Earth, I too could dive headlong into the world's problems and be a changemaker.

As we read the piece, we behold a precocious young man finding his way in the world, but at the same time possessing the judgment to seek counsel from great minds of yore.

Perspective

THE DENSITY OF INSIGHT IN THIS piece rivals articles written by professional essayists. Appreciating both a computer science concept (the *Library of Babel*) and the Hebrew myth from which it's derived requires profound knowledge in both the sciences and the humanities. Again, we see evidence of the "liberal arts mindset," or the ability to forge ideas from contrasting disciplines. Aditya can at once code and probe the "profound truth" contained within the parable, resolving not to repeat those mistakes in his own initiatives.

But this isn't a one-time spark! Aditya is constantly conversing with authors from diverse genres and eras, resulting in "far-away journeys through space and time, philosophical epiphanies, and friendships with unexpected characters." These aren't just stories, however; Aditya

proceeds to compare and contrast the idyllic scenes of Ruskin Bond
novels with the reality of rural life in modern India. He contextualizes
Mr. Bond's perspectives and implicitly recognizes how the Indian
landscape may have changed. He respects every one of their works, but
possesses the courage to question their conclusions.

While discussing *Brave New World*, Aditya wonders whether we've
arrived at the drug-induced dystopia the author depicted nearly a
century ago. Can social media be compared to soma? The way Aditya
presents his thoughts, we're certain that he doesn't read merely for
pleasure. His brain is constantly processing the words, determining
the extent to which they hold true. We're reminded here of Mortimer
Adler's timeless classic, *How to Read a Book*, in which he outlines four
general questions every reader must ask:

What is the author saying?

What is their evidence?

Is it true?

What of it?

Many stop at 1, some at 2 or 3. Few ask all four and invest the mental
effort to answer them. Reading and thinking are hard, especially if
you're in active conversation with humanity's vast intellectual heritage.
Nevertheless, that's precisely what elite universities are looking for:
young people devoted to broadening their horizons—and those of
humanity as a whole. And Aditya has already begun that journey:
"Through *Khetibaat*, I'm expanding my bookshelf, making it accessible
to millions of farmers, an agricultural Library of Babel." Bringing the
conversation full circle!

Authenticity

ADITYA, FAR FROM A CUSTOMARY TECHIE, remains continuously
engaged with the world around him. His knowledge comes not just
from screens and numbers, but also from current events. Such events
aren't always pleasant, and this young man must even come to terms
with the unsettling trend of farmer suicides pervading the Indian
hinterland.

As intelligent as he is, he's never overly sure of himself. Despite
his passion for computer science, he's not above questioning his own
"technophilia." (Note also that despite his pride in being a collector,

he's not above admitting, "My collection is neither fancy...nor as extensive as the Library of Babel.") In other words, all these lines reveal that Aditya Mehta is willing to acknowledge the world's complexity, and that he doesn't have all the answers. But that's okay; in fact, that's ideal. One must empty their cup before they can draw water from fresh springs. That's precisely what receiving a college education is like.

Craft

THE VERY FIRST LINE REFERS TO Babel; we naturally conclude that Aditya is one erudite kid—techie or not! This conclusion is reinforced throughout the piece, as he artfully introduces themes from unexpected texts, as though he were facilitating dialogues between them. This is an extremely advanced intellectual skill, one that academic circles especially prize.

While we're served a delectable dish, we also receive tangy condiments that enhance its flavor! The humorous asides provide insight into the kind of student Aditya will be on campus, even poking fun at his nerdy passions with phrases like, "beyond turning unsuspecting children into lifelong nerds destined to heated online debates on why the Fellowship couldn't just "fly the eagles to Mordor."

And on top of that, there are several examples of just beautiful, beautiful language. We'll present just one of our favorites here:

> As I had witnessed first-hand, Indian farmers too possess an intergenerational knowledge of the fields in which they toil. However, as if afflicted by Babel's curse, successful practices of a particular community remain within its linguistic borders, failing to pollinate other regions.

And thus, we have a truly stellar piece, a complete bildungsroman in 650 words. With this level of demonstrated depth and diversity of thought, it's no wonder Caltech came calling.

EXERCISE

Name a character from a book, movie, or TV show that exhibits characteristics that you wish to emulate. In what daily situations can you incorporate their spirit?

Workbook

Total Time Required: 10–20 hours

Total Drafts Required: 3–5

MATERIALS NEEDED

- **Official Essay Prompts (Available on the Common App Website and/or Portal)**
- **Activity List (Or Resume)**
- **Laptop or Pen/Pencil and Paper**

ALRIGHTY, SCHOLAR! CONGRATS ON MAKING IT through the contents of this book. By now, you've not only read 25 amazing essays, but also understood what makes them come alive and cause admissions officers to exclaim, "I want this candidate on my campus!"

But knowledge alone is incomplete without action. That's why, in this final chapter, we're going to share with you a comprehensive, step-by-step guide for how you can produce your own stellar Personal Essay. From our experience, there are three simple stages: **Ideation**, **Drafting**, and **Finalization**. To use a woodcutting metaphor, think of them as blueprinting, carving, and polishing. From end to end, it should take you anywhere from a week to a month (or maybe a few months if you really want to let the process marinate).

Remember: all writing requires serious thinking. Get yourself into the right headspace by finding a quiet environment with no distractions. Let's dig in!

GOAL = execute an effective Personal Essay that appeals to your specific audience and helps earn you admission to an Ivy League school.

Common Problems:
- Ignorance of audience's expectations
- Conservative, cliché approach to both subject matter and voice
- Poor writing skill
- Insufficient time given to the task

151

IDEATION

Time Required: 3-4 hours

WHAT WE LIKE TO CALL THE "Ideation" stage is the first macro stage of the Application Essay process, and arguably the most important. It involves the process of identifying the most compelling ideas, themes, and approaches that will best showcase your profile and ultimately produce a quality final draft. This is your foundation: without it, you're lost, as is your reader. Consequently, the piece will be weaker and require more revisions—even re-ideations. (Just try building a house without a foundation!) Hence, you should really take your time here. No need to rush. That said, we advise you not to get stuck in Ideation. Take your time to do it right, but then get moving.

There are three primary substages involved in Ideation: Planning, Brainstorming, and Outlining. These components may occur separately or simultaneously, as they can easily blend together.

GOAL = execute an effective Idea and Outline that you can ultimately use to produce a quality final draft.

Common Problems:
- Myopic vision (or lack thereof)
- Excessive overlap in themes between Personal Essay and Supplements
- Rushing into Brainstorming/Drafting without a clear sense of what to showcase about one's profile

152

Planning

SO, YOU THOUGHT YOU WERE JUST going to jump into the essay process blind, did you? Wrong! Have we learned nothing from the essays covered in the previous sections? Crafting the ideal Personal Essay doesn't occur by happenstance. It requires strategy. Hence, "Planning" is the process of identifying an effective theme and strategy for your application writing. There's a macro aspect and a micro aspect to the process. You must understand your audience (American college admissions officers) as well as the prompt(s)—especially the constraints, like word/character/page limit—and your scholar's profile. Without a grasp of these elements, you have no idea what you're supposed to be showcasing through your essay. The whole process will thus feel hopelessly ambiguous and confusing. So, before beginning the writing process in earnest, you must first identify the vision.

1. Identify what kinds of essays and other components you'll need to submit for your applications. Most American schools are on the Common App, which features a long-form 650-word Personal Essay that's general to all schools. The Coalition App functions similarly. Visit the website and study the prompts, as well as the specific Supplements and other application components. The Personal Essay prompts for the current application cycle are typically released by January or February, as to give you time to ponder them. The Supplements are typically released in August, but you can generally expect that most schools will require at least one additional essay beyond the Personal Essay—perhaps a question about your intended major or why you want to attend.

    Since the Supplements are so topical, usually involving discussion of your academic interests and community service efforts, it's smart to avoid these themes in your Personal Essay—or at least to keep them brief so that you can write about them in-depth in your Supplements without coming off repetitive. You never want to be a one-trick pony, for such an image will likely appear boring to your reader. Instead, use each essay type (as well as the other application components) to showcase another facet of what makes you a compelling candidate. In the consulting world, they call this approach MECE, or mutually exclusive, collectively exhaustive. Each component of your application should be essentially distinct in showcasing unique elements of your profile and Character/Personal Qualities; simultaneously, it should add up with each other application component in such a way that covers everything noteworthy about your profile and Character/Personal Qualities. Your goal is to present a cohesive, comprehensive theme throughout your application while also presenting its diversity. Think both depth *and* breadth.

2. Specify a timeline for when you want to complete each stage of the writing progress. This helps to keep you on track. Having a plan gives you structure. It keeps you accountable (particularly if you obtain help from a friend or family member).

3. Before you truly begin your essay process, the first thing to do is to understand the human brand you wish to convey to admissions officers! Are you the tech-savvy computer scientist who also loves to perform in plays? Are you the literature-loving reader who just so happens to be a mathlete? Think about the traits and activities that make you interesting to your admissions audience. Note them down and identify in one line what constitutes your personal brand. Think then about how you can upend the reader's expectations through antistereotyping.

Brainstorming

NOW THINGS GET EXCITING. BRAINSTORMING IS the process of establishing the big-picture Content, Structure, and Style for your Personal Essay—in other words, an idea. If planning is the compass that provides you with much-needed direction, then brainstorming is experimentation with how to actually get there. It involves a ton of trial and error, just like science. Everyone's approach will be different, so try out ideas. Trust us, there's no One Idea that will make everything perfect. You're not trying to find something so much as you're trying to create it. There could be multiple great options. And guess what? That's what the Supplements are for. If you end up with so much awesome material that you can't fit it all in the Personal Essay, just save it for the other essays! Most students (typically Type-A perfectionists) struggle because they think they must get everything right from the start. Well, "right" is alright, but the best work arises from happy accidents. Do you think all classic books or movies went completely according to plan?

Common Problems:
- Closed-minded thinking
- Excessive self-criticism, thus blocking the flow of ideas
- Failure to write down one's thoughts (thus forgetting good ideas)

1. Find yourself a nice, quiet space and open up a blank document (or a blank sheet of paper, if you like). Silence your phone and notifications (perhaps leave unnecessary devices in another room entirely). Cultivate an environment conducive to introspection and creativity. It's difficult to think and write well when you face distractions.

2. Review the official Personal Essay prompts, and decide which ones appeal to you most. Place them on your document or sheet of paper.

   Students frequently find that the open-endedness of the Personal Essay feels intimidating; therefore, they need structure. Brainstorming for a specific prompt helps you aim toward a target. The poet Robert Frost famously dismissed free verse as akin to "playing tennis without a net." Just as he preferred to rely on traditional structures such as meter and rhyme to compose his verses, you can let the prompts be your "net."

3. Complete as many of the exercises featured at the end of each essay commentary as possible. This will get your ideas flowing and unlock content seeds that you can nourish into mighty trees!

   (Keep in mind the most common Personal Essay topics. The ideas you come up with may indeed feel unique to you, but in reality, they're likely cliché. That's why you need to really keep your ideas specific to your own distinct lived experience and perspective.

Most Common Topics

- Family member (especially parents or grandparents)
- Bullying
- School organization/club
- Personal project (volunteering)
- Sports (captainship, injury)
- Relocation (e.g. changing schools)
- Travel

As you can see, the general topics that arise each year are by and large predictable. This situation is understandable, as most students who apply to college have had similar lived experiences. AOs are well aware. They don't necessarily expect you to come up with the most unusual topics as much as they expect you to have something interesting and meaningful to say about your distinct vantage point. Common topics are merely genres, just as books and films have genres, such as action/adventure, thriller, comedy, romance, sci-fi, and so on. What keeps things fresh is how you play with genres to arrive at something new. That's the definition of creativity. In other words, no need to avoid genre; just be aware that it exists. Know the conventions so you can upend them!

4. Based on your responses to the exercises above, brainstorm 10 potential Personal Essay topics.

5. Experiment with different Brainstorming techniques, according to whatever works for you. Some like blue-sky thinking (completely open-ended thoughts). Some prefer what we call the "Octopus method," beginning with one central image or topic and using word associations that stem outward from the center like tentacles. One of our favorites is aptly named "10 Bad Ideas," which asks you to quickly list the first 10 thoughts that come to your head, avoiding judgment or self-criticism. The first couple will likely be terrible, which is fine, but once you reach the seventh or eighth, you start to reach the gold. It's a fine way to reduce the self-induced pressure of getting the first idea right.

6. Feel free to discuss your responses with parents, siblings, friends, and even teachers! Sounding boards are essential to generating, developing, and refining ideas so they're fit to share with the world. Just beware over-critiquing your ideas before you've given them a chance to breathe. It's like nipping a flower in the bud.

7. From the above 10, shortlist your three favorites. (Remember: you'll likely need to write additional essays asked by each college, so don't worry if you find yourself struggling to choose!)

Outlining

SO, THE PLANNING SUBSTAGE WAS IDENTIFYING the need, and the Brainstorming substage was identifying potential approaches. Outlining, then, is the final substage before you actually begin building. The Outline serves as a blueprint for the writing piece; it is the Structure upon which everything else stands. It establishes your theme and/or thesis, along with the organization of ideas that precipitates an effective introduction all the way to a satisfying conclusion. If the Planning and Brainstorming comprise the compass, then the Outline is the map.

Beware: there's a sweet spot for the level of detail your Outline should contain. Too much elaboration, and you'll snuff the spark of your initial idea (this is one case where the architecture adage, "Measure once, cut twice" doesn't exactly apply!). Too little, and you risk a flimsy Structure. Approach the Outline according to your personal affinities and skills. Some writers depend on the sense of guidance that a thorough Outline gives; others merely need the slightest inkling of a shape to build their grand edifice. Our best suggestion is to be sturdy without being rigid, flexible without being weak.

Common Problems:
- Disorganized ideas
- Overly detailed, thus rigid Outline (that later produces stale, uncreative draft)
- Overambitious ("overstuffed") Outline featuring too many ideas and narrative threads

- Underdeveloped, thus loose Outline (that later produces nonsensical, unimpactful draft)

1. For each of the three ideas you shortlisted, identify a "logline." In the film and publishing industry, a logline is a sentence or two that boils down the script to its essential elements in the form of a concise summary:

Who's the protagonist? (In this case, you!)

What conflict do they face?

How do they overcome that conflict?

How do they grow in that process?

Do all these fancy terms sound vague or mysterious to you? How about we break them down. First, a "protagonist," or "hero," is simply the main character in a narrative. They may or may not be all that heroic per se, but they're the person we focus on the most, usually because the story presents the world through their eyes (think Luke Skywalker or Harry Potter). As a result, we as readers (or viewers or listeners) become attached to the protagonist's perspective and come to care about them. This is your goal with any college Application Essay!

Of course, a protagonist hardly exists without an antagonist. Essentially synonymous with "villain," "enemy," or "adversary," "antagonist" simply means against the protagonist. We typically think of the antagonist as a human being—like Darth Vader or Lord Voldemort—but it can just as easily be a beast, robot, or something more abstract. In fact, we'd argue that the real antagonist in any story is almost always something internal, not external. Luke Skywalker, for example, must conquer the physical threat of Darth Vader, who wishes for tyranny throughout the universe, but deeper, he must conquer his own relationship to good and evil. Similarly, Harry Potter must defeat the sinister Lord Voldemort, but He Who Shall Not Be Named is merely a manifestation of the doubts and fears that Harry faces within.

When a protagonist struggles with such opposing forces—beliefs, values, perspectives, opportunities—they're wrestling with a *conflict*. Often, a conflict is interpersonal, meaning that it results from disagreements or frustrations with at least one other person, but just as often, it can be intrapersonal, meaning that it results from disagreements or frustrations with *oneself*. Our existence is defined by relationships, with others and with ourselves, which makes conflict such a universal facet of storytelling. As human beings, we're bound to come into conflict, whether big (as in, saving the universe) or small (as in, leading your football team). Admissions officers don't care if you write about something grand or something mundane; they simply care about you having something to say. Just look at the CAE prompts. Several discuss problems you faced or changes you made. If you have a conflict, the expectation is that you'll eventually resolve it. If you were successful, what change occurred? What new perspectives do you have now? How have you grown? These kinds of questions apply to stories of all kinds. In the case of Luke Skywalker, we can see that he's learned to integrate the Light Side and the Dark Side of the Force. He seems more mature now. As does Harry at the end of his narrative. When you look to the essays featured in the previous chapters, do you feel that the protagonists have also grown?

Note: your essay need not be a *story*, as in a narrative that portrays past events in chronological order. You could just as easily discuss something that fascinates you (CAE prompt #6) or bothers you. It could be a day in your life, a rant, a parody, even a poem. Similarly, your "conflict" need not be resolved completely by the end. Perhaps it's an ongoing journey or challenge—this is good and fine! After all, admissions departments primarily care about your *potential*. If you had everything already figured out, there'd be no reason to go to college!

You can write your loglines here!

2. Choose one of the three loglines above and expand it into an outline. Our preferred method is to list 3–5 main bullet points, each highlighting the content of a respective paragraph. Although the standard 5-paragraph essay format that schools often teach has limits (e.g. formulaic approach, redundant conclusion), it can be quite helpful as a framework to guide you. Any interesting, worthwhile story will generally progress in terms of plot, theme, and so on, which means that in some form, you'll need an attention-grabbing opener (what writers often call a "hook") that sets up the point of the essay, some significant developments that build on this purpose, and finally, a means of tying up the loose ends of your discussion. What does that sound like? A five-paragraph essay: Introduction (1), Body Paragraphs (3), Conclusion (1).

To ground your Outline, start with your logline. It serves as your theme. If your story is about x, for example, think about how this narrative would take shape in the form of actual paragraphs. A 650-word Personal Essay will generally comprise about 7–8 average-length paragraphs of 4–5 sentences or 75 words each. A simple framework we love to use is called MAL*, or Motivation-Action-Learning. It applies to both the overall essay Structure as well as the structure of each paragraph. Any story features a "Motivation," as in a problem, conflict, or inciting incident that sets its plot in motion. A personal motivation is almost always rooted in a desire, such as Athena scholar Aastha Tiwari's wish to reconcile science and art. It tends to reflect one's Values, as only a kid who cares deeply about intellectual questions of science and art would strive to reconcile them in the first place. You might imagine, then, that "Motivation" tends to come in the beginning, during the introduction (in this case, the "Abstract" and "Hypothesis" sections). "Action," of course, is the plot moving along; it's the events and deeds that complicate the theme and advance the narrative toward its conclusion. For Aastha, it's the humorous investigation and testing of her hypothesis. We like to call this process of plot and character development "escalation." Last, "Learning" accounts for whatever lessons the protagonist might've gained. Aastha, in her "Results" and "Conclusions" sections, learns that her hypothesis was incorrect. Such insights lend themselves well to an essay's conclusion, bringing the whole piece full circle.

Still, MAL can also apply to each specific paragraph of an essay. Your opening, or "topic" sentence serves to introduce the reader to the purpose and claim of the paragraph. The body sentences build from that idea, and your concluding sentence ties it up while pivoting the reader toward the next paragraph. When you think in this way, "transitions" between paragraphs make much more sense, and it's far easier to know what to write at any given point of the narrative.

REVIEW YOUR OUTLINE. DOES IT CONTAIN the essential elements of Values, Perspective, Authenticity, and Craft? If not, how can you better introduce or emphasize them?

DRAFTING

Time Required: 6–12 hours
Drafts Required: 2–4

NOW YOU'RE READY TO WRITE! THE Drafting stage is the second and middle macro stage of the Application Essay writing process—usually the longest. The challenge is to compose a quality draft of your writing piece that can then be finalized as the final version of the essay you'll submit for your application. Most applicants struggle with this stage the most, as they typically lack literary skill. It goes without saying that most people *in general* are unskilled at writing, but this challenge is especially critical for Asian applicants, who're usually trained by education systems that prioritize STEM and quantitative assessment over the liberal arts focus of the American system. Add to that a rising trend away from reading books, and you have a population unaware of how to express themselves on paper in an interesting, compelling manner.

But nonetheless, draft you must. It's the only way to one day arrive at a final essay. (Remember: generative AI like ChatGPT is resoundingly discouraged by virtually all colleges when it comes to Drafting!) Expect your essay to go through multiple drafts; hardly no one ever gets it "right" the first time. There's nothing wrong with that! With each draft, your essay should ideally improve.

There are three primary sub stages involved in Ideation: First Draft, Feedback, and Revision. These components may occur separately or simultaneously, as they can easily blend together.

GOAL = execute an effective Draft that you can ultimately use to produce a quality final draft

Common Problems:

- Procrastination or failure to finish drafts
- Superficial or uninteresting Content
- Incoherence or failure to adhere to Outline Structure
- Boring or generic literary voice (Style)
- Unreadable text due to poor grammar, punctuation, and formatting (Mechanics)

First Draft

OBVIOUSLY, THE FIRST DRAFT IS YOUR first tangible deliverable for any given essay. It marks the official transition from Ideation (Outlining) to Drafting stage, thus giving the team a stronger sense of where the scholar stands and how much work will subsequently be needed. Often, it's the most difficult substage, because the Ideation stage is generally quite broad and fun, requiring comparatively minimal actual writing effort. The First Draft, in contrast, requires genuine, sustained thought, using a skill that most applicants have yet to master. In this way, the First Draft is where the rubber hits the road. It's translating theory into practice. The best laid plans of the Ideation stage must ultimately face the realities of your own human limitations. For many applicants, this fact is too great to bear, which makes them procrastinate the process indefinitely. Caught up in their perfectionism, they develop so much fear that they find the only way to avoid arriving at a non-ideal draft is to avoid writing altogether.

Don't be that kid! Instead, remind yourself that the first draft is rarely the *last* draft. It's a foundation, and nothing more. In fact, that very foundation often gets replaced with a better one, so you don't even have to remain attached to a draft that you don't like. The key is just getting *something* out, so you can see where you stand. Take from the field of design, in which workers are asked to produce an **MVP**, or minimum viable product. There'll be several later iterations of that initial product, but those can't exist until something precedes them.

Think of your First Draft as your prototype. It's a proof of concept for your idea. Would you rather have a working, if flawed prototype, or a perfect but unrealized schematic?

GOAL = produce a first draft of sufficient quality that you can go on to effectively finalize without excessive Revision

Common Problems:

- Failure to begin or finish (procrastination, perfectionism)
- Overly short draft (that's therefore unuseful)
- Overly long draft (that's therefore difficult to parse)
- Disorganized ideas

1. Set a timer (anywhere from 60 to 120 minutes) and— guided by your Outline—write from the heart. Don't worry about Style or Mechanics. Similarly, don't worry about length. Just focus on conveying your story and message in the most honest, direct way possible. And don't succumb to perfectionism! Get your ideas down, so you can then proceed to edit, polish, and finalize them. Write one word, one sentence, one paragraph at a time. This is how things get done: one step at a time. Flesh out the points you wish to make so that at least the Content is all present. Once you have that, deepening, restructuring, and so forth are easy.

   If you're struggling with the above, we recommend a 15-minute freewriting exercise. Again, set a timer and write WHATEVER comes to your mind. It doesn't have to be related to a topic. It doesn't have to make sense. It doesn't even have to be in English. The goal is to relax your filter and stop self-censoring, so your subconscious magnificence can emerge onto the page. Be experimental. Be wacky. Enjoy yourself. This process is supposed to be enjoyable. If your draft reflects playfulness, that energy is infectious. It'll rub off on the reader.

   Remember: for some writers, expressing themselves comes naturally. Their primary struggle is coming up with too much content, or too many ideas—none of which may be substantive or coherent. For some writers, expressing themselves is extremely difficult. It takes them ages just to put one word down to paper.

Wherever on the spectrum you fall, be true to yourself. This is why you set aside time well ahead of the deadline to get your essay right. Unfortunately, the added pressure of waiting to the last minute only makes these obstacles greater.

Feedback

FEEDBACK IS THE PROCESS OF OBTAINING perspective and guidance from others so you can then revise your writing piece and ultimately produce a compelling final draft. All writing can be improved with the help of fresh eyes. Our readers see the blind spots that we, the writers, cannot. Soliciting feedback, then, is the closest thing you have to simulating your AO's reading experience. What you seek is an objective lens to counter your own subjectivity; if a reader pinpoints something you missed, then you might've been a bit myopic.

GOAL = efficiently obtain perspective and guidance to revise one's draft into a quality draft that can then be finalized

Common Problems:

- Seeking Feedback too soon or too late
- Pride and arrogance preventing openness to Feedback
- Passive acceptance of Feedback (thus diluting personal literary voice)
- Too many inputs from too many perspectives (thus producing incoherent Content/Structure/Style and/or diluted personal literary voice)

1. Identify when it's time to share your draft with others for Feedback. Writing is an intensely personal exercise—they don't call it the "Personal Essay" for nothing—so you'll have to be the judge for when it's appropriate to welcome the world in. You don't have to do it all at once. Just as many literary writers have a primary editor with whom they've built a strong, trusting relationship, you may have a single friend or family member (like a parent or sibling) whom you would want to see your essay in its raw, unedited form (especially if it's about a sensitive subject). This one person may be the only one you can rely on to give their honest, candid take. They may be privy to the

draft's text long before others get to see it, and that's a perfectly acceptable approach. Find the right sweet spot: you want to be protective of your vision, but also open enough to refine it.

2. Once you've completed a draft that you're ready to share for feedback, select your reader(s) and request their support. This is a place where audience and authority really do matter. While your friends and family may have your best interests at heart, they may not be fully qualified to know what works and what doesn't in a Personal essay for college. Most people who have no experience in the field come with a host of misguided expectations about what a "Application Essay" is supposed to be. You'll find this ignorance even more pronounced in cultures unaccustomed to America's holistic, liberal arts-centric admissions system. Because those trained to write SOPs and take STEM exams often have no insight into other systems, they may push you to be conservative in your approach. Be careful! Remind them that there are no "rules" to the process. If you need to, consult official admissions websites, which explicitly state their expectations for Personal Essays. Opinions will be subjective. Keep your external readers to a minimum—maybe 3–4 individuals—as to avoid having a problem of "too many cooks in the kitchen."

    Also, be sure to keep your request clear (e.g. soliciting comments versus edits) and respect your reader's time. 650 words is a significant amount of text to sift through. Be patient and understanding if someone doesn't have the bandwidth to help at the moment. Written Feedback is almost always more useful than spoken Feedback, so get your readers to relay their comments on paper. That way, you can refer to them later without relying solely on memory. If someone shares harsh feedback, ask them to keep their perspective constructive instead of destructive. You shouldn't shy away from honesty, but you shouldn't have to take abuse either. The writing process is supposed to be fun—it's supposed to make you feel good!

Revision

REVISION IS ESSENTIALLY THE FINAL DRAFTING substage, but in actuality, it'll likely go in tandem with Feedback. The two substages form a feedback loop. The danger of Revision is that it's necessary, but quite amorphous. Who's to say when an essay is finally "done"? Ostensibly, you could keep editing it forever. Hence, for many scholars, each subsequent draft following the first produces diminishing returns, as they lack a mature understanding of how to concretely improve their drafts. Meanwhile, external readers typically struggle to communicate their perspective, a situation that produces ongoing confusion. There's a reason why it's said that "the creative work is never finished; it is abandoned."

Remember: great writing is rewriting, so don't be disappointed if you have to go back and tweak a few items. With every edit, you're becoming a better thinker and communicator.

GOAL = produce a draft of sufficient quality that you can go on to effectively finalize

Common Problems:

- Underediting (i.e. too few revisions, resulting in an unpolished final draft)
- Overediting (i.e. too many revisions, thanks to perfectionism)
- Careless editing (missed transitions between paragraphs, etc.)
- Rushing each iteration
- Myopia (excessive focus on minute details or word limit instead of overall impact)

1. Ignoring concerns of word limit, give your essay one edit yourself, asking whether the Values, Perspective, Authenticity, and Craft are shining through (by now, you should be a pro!). Are the Content and Structure conveying what you truly wish to say? Does the Style reflect your true, authentic voice? If not, you still need additional inputs.

   Don't be afraid to make drastic changes. One of the great challenges applicants face is getting locked into one idea or approach that isn't really working. Sometimes, the very subject matter itself is the problem. Sometimes, it's the choice of voice— for instance, one Athena applicant eventually had to replace third-person perspective with the more traditional first-person because the former was coming off too pretentious. That said, don't give up on unconventional ideas too quickly, either. Too frequently, writers discard great approaches that have potential, finding that it was too difficult to execute them, or someone's Feedback was negative toward them. If you have something you believe in, fight for it! Retain the good elements and remove the bad. Don't throw the baby out with the bathwater!

In this early phase (drafts 1–3), your focus should be on the big picture, what we at Athena like to call the "Helicopter View." If you were to zoom out and view your essay from high up "in a helicopter," what would you see? Each detail of the essay may be important, but only in as much as it builds with the next into a cohesive whole. Your initial edits should thus be concerned with identifying which plot elements should be kept/developed, which characters. If the conclusion is too superficial, elaborate it. If there's missing context for something important that you mention, clarify it for the reader. You can always reduce the Content afterward.

2. Incorporate Feedback from your trusted friends, family, and/or mentors. Pay close attention to the specific word choices they used. When you finish your revisions, ask yourself whether you actually addressed their Feedback.

3. Now, print out your draft and read it with "Admissions Officer glasses," assessing whether this is a young person you'd love to interact with on an elite American college campus. If not, what qualities are missing? How can you bring those out?

4. Once you're ready for the true refinement phase (drafts 3–4), it's time to introduce a paradigm shift. Instead of adding, you're now subtracting. Most likely, you've still got a draft that's well above the word limit, which means that some significant cuts will be needed. This is well and good. Once you finish, you'll see that none of these bits was strictly necessary anyway. Just as a movie must be edited down for a manageable runtime, an essay must be edited down to an acceptable length.

Here's a useful framework:

When you're still around 25%+ over the word limit (around 800+ words for a 650-word essay), your problem is mainly structural. You need to remove large chunks of text (usually entire anecdotes and/or characters). Ask yourself, if I delete this whole paragraph, will the narrative still make sense?

When you're less than 25% over the word limit (less than 800 words for a 650-word essay), your problem is mainly language. You need to make your sentences more concise. This is now the realm of line editing, wherein we replace wordy phrases and unnecessary modifiers for simpler, more straightforward statements. Ask yourself, can this idea be conveyed in one sentence instead of two?

One of our favorite techniques is to color code sections of the essay according to MAL. Go ahead and highlight all sentences that fit under "M" with one color, "A" with another, and "L" with a third. If you discover that 75% of the essay is Motivation, for example, then clearly, you've got a tone of buildup with only minimal development and payoff. Most likely, you'll want to reduce some of the M.

In your first major refinement edit, slash away at the big items mentioned at the top, then in your second, address the details mentioned at the bottom. If you reverse the order, you'll get bogged down in the intricacies of language, a vain exercise when it's premature. You won't be able to see the forest for the trees. Before you know it, you'll be under your word limit!

FINALIZATION

Time Required: 2-4 hours

IN MANY WAYS, THE FINAL STAGE is the most important. Universities routinely ask that essays be free from all errors. And why not? Sloppiness reflects poorly on your character. Who wants to read an essay that's littered with grammatical, spelling, punctuation, or formatting mistakes? If the admissions officer is akin to a future employer, and you're the candidate, they have to base their opinion of your potential on whether you present yourself as a professional. This is where Craft comes in. It's not just "Style" or "Mechanics" per se. It's the care with which you approach your writing. Submissions that are well proofread convey meticulousness on the part of the author—in other words, maturity.

Of course, there's another side to the finalization stage that must also be mentioned. Some authors, terrified of having their work be imperfect (which would thus make them appear imperfect), struggle to simply finish their draft. It may be cleanly edited and ready to go, but they'll still insist on tweaking it. This tendency, though sometimes admirable, can lead to paralysis. That old line returns: the creative work is never finished; it is abandoned. Submit your best work, but don't let your desire for greatness lead to inaction!

Common Problems:

- Formatting: chances are, your application portal will look quite different from your word processor. It may not preserve all the formatting choices you've made, such as italics, bold, underline, indentation, or alignment. Always check by testing the portal first. One scholar attempted to quote a Punjabi excerpt in her CAE only to find that Punjabi characters wouldn't be supported!

- Inconsistency: many applicants will have a Personal Essay in one dialect (such as American English), but the remaining application components in another (British English). Don't just think in terms of your primary essay but rather in terms of your application as a whole.

- Gimmicks: excessive emphasis (bold, italics, underline) or clunky organization (too many short/long paragraphs) can be distracting and even frustrating for your reader. Remember that your core focus is readability. Make things easy for the admissions officer. The reading experience should be a pleasurable, entertaining one. Aesthetics are important!

1. Reread your essay aloud, ensuring that all statements are clear, transitions between ideas make sense, and intended details have been addressed. Scrutinize the text for all grammatical and typographical errors (spelling, punctuation, formatting). You're now donning the role of copy editor, so review your work as an objective third party. And what's the primary concern for a copy editor? Establishing clarity.

2. It's said that proofreading is made difficult when you read quietly and/or use a screen, as the eyes and brain are lulled into a false sense of comfort. To counteract this bias, again print out your draft and read the hard copy aloud. You'll be surprised at the errors you spot. Even better, reread your draft from bottom-up. This technique helps to verify that transitions between ideas have been thoroughly established. Because your brain must operate more attentively to understand the narrative backwards, you'll be more likely to spot lapses.

3. Ensure that you remain consistent with British or American spelling. We at Athena recommend that you use British English for British schools, American for American ones, and so on. It's just a matter of speaking your audience's language. This approach is optional, of course. Whichever dialect you

choose, be consistent! Align all components of your application (including Personal Information, Activity List, etc.) with the same English conventions, else risk the effect of appearing disjointed. (Admissions departments are well aware that many affluent applicants use external guidance; as a result, they most certainly expect those applicants to be all the more rigorous about such discrepancies.)

4. Have someone you trust help you give it one final read aloud, then go ahead and submit!

GLOSSARY

- **ACADEMIC PROFILE**

  Among the several basic admissions profile types that exist, the Academic Profile is defined by an emphasis on pursuing one's intellectual passion through co-curricular excellence in the form of independent coursework, olympiads, and research. A prime example would be Harsh Dutta's CAE, centered on his obsession with physics.

- **ACTIVITY LIST**

  The Activity List is a central component for your undergraduate application, highlighting a set number of activities, responsibilities, and hobbies you engage in, along with your positions and time commitment. Most undergraduate applications will feature some form of Activity List, which functions essentially as your resume. If college admissions is like recruitment for a job—i.e. the position of Student—then colleges want to know what you've accomplished during your high-school career. They need to see the facts, figures, and achievements.

- **ADMISSIONS OFFICER (AO)**

  An admissions officer is an employee of a university's admissions department tasked with the responsibility of recruiting, evaluating, and/or selecting prospective students for each incoming class. Part-recruiter, part-talent scout, part-agent, and part-advocate, an admissions officer serves as one of the gatekeepers to a university's enrolled student body. AOs rarely operate alone, however; because they belong to a department, they work in collaboration with fellow AOs. Depending on your intended school, your application may be read by at least two AOs, followed by a committee. Demographically, AOs may come from any nationality, religion, gender, race/ethnicity, sexual identity, or socioeconomic status. The AO who reads your application will generally be responsible for all applicants from your geographical region.

- **APPLICATION ESSAY**

   An Application Essay is an essay asked by a college application. An umbrella term, it represents a wide genre of college essay writing that includes the Personal Essay as well as the statement of purpose (SOP), Supplements, and more. Typically, an Application Essay will feature a prompt (with one or more sub-questions) and a word, character, line, and/or page limit. This book is primarily focused on the Personal Essay genre.

- **APPLICATION PLATFORM**

   An application platform is an application system that helps a university and its applicants manage the application process. Some are native applications designed and managed for one institution, e.g. the University of California (UC) app, MIT application, Georgetown application, ApplyTexas (UT Austin), MyIllini (UIUC), while others are designed and managed for multiple institutions instead of just one (e.g. Common App, Coalition Application, QuestBridge).

- **ANTISTEREOTYPING**

   Possibly coined by admissions expert Pria Chatterjee, antistereotyping is the act of subverting the stereotypes of your admissions Baskets, thus generating hooks and interest. For example, an Indian male physics student like Ish Kaul wouldn't be expected to have a deep beatboxing interest, so the reader becomes immediately curious to read more. His brand is therefore more distinct than that of a peer who merely plays into STEM stereotypes.

- **AUTHENTICITY**

  Within our VPAC framework, Authenticity is the third priority, defined by honesty, genuineness, and vulnerability. A successful Personal Essay must be appropriately candid, else it will fall flat, hollow, or impersonal.

- **BASKET**

  Possibly coined by admissions expert Pria Chatterjee, a Basket is one of the descriptive categories that admissions departments use to group and evaluate applicants. There are 9 main Baskets that applicants can fall into: 6 are uncontrollable ("Demographics"), while the remaining 3 are controllable ("Interests").

  ### Demographics (Uncontrollable)
  - Race/Ethnicity
  - Gender
  - Geographic Location
  - Citizenship
  - Income Level
  - Alumni Relation (Legacy)

  ### Interests (Controllable, aka the "Three A's")
  - Academics (including field of study)
  - Athletics
  - Activities

- **CHARACTER DEVELOPMENT**

  In narrative writing, character development is the portrayal of a character's growth and evolution over time. Usually, it's a reflection of maturation. Said character is said to go through a "character arc," from perhaps stuck-up and prim like Hermione Granger to something much more likable by the end of the series. To demonstrate character development—for yourself or others—in a Personal Essay can be a great way to endear your reader to yourself or others.

- **CHARACTER/PERSONAL QUALITIES**

  Admissions departments seek a certain set of Character/Personal Qualities in their candidates. These traits reflect American values broadly, but can also be specific to an individual college. For example, essentially all admissions departments prize these standard five Character/Personal Qualities—Intellectual

Vitality, Community/Diversity Orientation, Leadership/ Ambition, Courage, and Tenacity—but some schools may emphasize certain ones more than others. Harvard is especially known for cultivating world leaders, while UChicago loves a risky thinker. Your goal for the Personal Essay is to showcase at least one of these traits.

- **COALITION APPLICATION**
  Founded in 2015, the Coalition Application is a standardized application platform akin to the Common App with a somewhat similar UI/UX and list of participating schools. It's hosted by the Coalition for College, formerly the Coalition for Access, Affordability, and Success, an American nonprofit organization. Its focus is on making the undergraduate application process easier for marginalized groups.
- **COALITION APPLICATION ESSAY**
  The Coalition Application Essay is the long-form 650-word Personal Essay that the Coalition App asks of all applicants. With similar prompts and a lack of college-specific focus, it's the Coalition App's analogue to the Common App's CAE.
- **COMMON APPLICATION (COMMON APP)**
  Founded in 1975, the Common Application is a standardized application platform akin to the Coalition App with a somewhat similar UI/UX and list of participating schools. It's hosted by the nonprofit organization of the same name. Of the many standardized application platforms that exist, the Common App is by far the most popular and widely accepted.
  Note: many people use "Common App" with reference to the "Common App Essay." Be clear whenever you use these terms interchangeably.
- **COMMON APP ESSAY (CAE)**
  The Common Application Essay (termed "Personal Essay" in the application itself) is the long-form 650-word Personal Essay that the Common App asks of all applicants. With similar prompts and a lack of college-specific focus, it's the Common App's analogue to the Coalition App's Coalition App Essay.
- **CONTENT**
  Within our Content, Structure, Style, and Mechanics framework, Content is the top priority, defined by an essay's

subject matter—in other words, its *substance*. A successful Personal Essay must be appropriately interesting and deep in its message, while showcasing your application Hooks. Otherwise, it'll appear superficial.

- **CRAFT**

  Within our VPAC framework, Craft is the final priority, defined by an essay's sense of Style. The term is synonymous with craftsmanship, as AOs wish to see applicants approach their essay with care and attention to detail. They don't need to be literary masterpieces, just artful in the author's own unique way. A successful Personal Essay must be appropriately creative—in topic, form, and/or language—otherwise, it'll appear generic.

- **CULTURAL ROOTEDNESS**

  Cultural Rootedness is an Athena Education coinage that simply signifies a student being consciously aware of their cultural background—race/ethnicity, religion, nationality, geographic context, etc.—and demonstrating appreciation of it. Admissions departments have really taken to the idea of "community" lately, with a special emphasis on DEI, or diversity, equity, and inclusion. They seek a class of diverse students who all bring unique perspectives from their respective traditions while respecting those of others. Applicants who are culturally rooted appear to demonstrate more Authenticity.

- **DISABILITY ESSAY**

  Within the set of the most common Personal Essay genres, the Disability Essay is defined by the author's diagnosis of a particular disability, condition, or disease. Avijan Chandhok's CAE, featured in the sample essays chapter, is a prime example. Common dangers include making the narrative into an unintentional sob story.

- **DIVERSITY**

  Diversity is among the most common buzzwords in today's admissions industry. Colleges seek to curate the most diverse classes possible, while nonetheless maintaining social harmony. They operate on a (rather American) idealistic philosophy that respectful pluralism produces the most innovative and enriching results, along with fairness, as traditionally marginalized groups receive representation in the population. Note that "Diversity" comes in, well, diverse forms: race/ethnicity, gender/sexual identity, ability, religion, political affiliation, just to name a few.

- **DO-GOODER ESSAY**

    Within the set of the most common Personal Essay genres, the Do-Gooder Essay is defined by the author's persona as someone who cares deeply about the less fortunate and engages in selfless service to make their world a better place. Navya Agarwal's CAE, featured in the sample essays chapter, is a prime example. When done right, the Do-Gooder Essay can demonstrate compelling Values of compassion, empathy, and orientation toward community. Common dangers include pretentiousness, self-importance, and phoniness.

- **ESCALATION**

    In narrative writing, escalation is the heightening of theme or the deepening of conflict toward some sort of impactful climax or conclusion. It's largely synonymous with the body paragraphs of an essay. Examples include the increasing challenges that Gaurvi Singhvi faces along her journey to cross the English Channel in her CAE. Escalation is a feature built into the Structure of any narrative; therefore, your Outline must account for it.

- **FIT**

    "Fit," or what we like to call "Alignment," is a highly subjective, qualitative concept in admissions used to evaluate an applicant's candidacy. If an applicant demonstrates Fit, then they seem to be a good match for the university's values and rigor. If not, the AO has reason to pause. This idea of holistic and contextual admissions is generally associated with the American model, which may be quite foreign to international applicants. With your Personal Essay, your goal is to prove to the reader that you really belong in the American education system because you align with its liberal arts philosophy and model, which also valorizes athletics and community engagement.

- **GENRE**

    "Genre" takes up many meanings, depending on the context. Broadly speaking, genre is a category of subject matter or style that defines a particular kind of work—e.g. action/adventure, thriller, comedy, or romance. This pattern establishes a certain set of well-understood expectations or conventions (such as the tropes of double-crossing in spy films, or jump scares in horror films) that can then be subverted playfully with some original storytelling. More specific to college essays is the idea of genre such as the Personal Essay vs. SOP vs. the Supplement. Also, within these essay genres may lie the sub-genres of the Do-Gooder Essay and Traumatic Experience Essay, among many more.

- **HOOK**

  "Hook" takes up several meanings, depending on the context. Broadly speaking, a hook is an attention-grabbing opener for a narrative work that draws the reader/viewer/listener in and makes them want to keep reading/watching/listening. For an Application Essay, that may be the whole first paragraph or just the initial lines. Common hooks include a short pithy one-line sentence as opening paragraph or asking a question.

  A more Application Essay-specific definition appears to derive from admissions consultant Pria Chatterjee, who defines a Hook by how an applicant may belong to an in-demand Basket, such as an openly queer male Indian applicant who studies archaeology.

- **HUMAN BRAND**

  In 2013, intellectuals Chris Malone and Susan Fiske released a book arguing that human societies must constantly evaluate members based on the unique combination of their "competence" and "warmth." Someone who's talented or otherwise reliable in a limited domain may lack warmth and thus build poor relationships. Meanwhile, someone who's full of emotional affect and compassion but lacks talent may lack respect from others. Having both gets you hired for jobs and admitted to colleges.

- **HUMBLEBRAG**

  A portmanteau of humble and brag, humblebrag sounds just like what it is. Unlike many Eastern education systems, which teach their students to avoid drawing attention to themselves, American admissions departments want to see you be self-aware of your accomplishments and cognizant of your value-add to their campus. The trick? You have to be at least somewhat *humble* about your individualistic pride. Otherwise, you'll just come off as a pompous jerk.

- **INTELLECTUAL ORIGINALITY**

  Intellectual Originality is a trait that defines cleverness, inventiveness, and creativity in an Application Essay.

- **INTENDED MAJOR**

  A loose term broadly encompassing the general field you seek to study in college (which you fill in the "Academics" section of your college application). While the major ("course" or "program") is almost always quite fixed in most parts of the world, like India or the UK, it's much more flexible in the States. Within the American system, students often may change majors after matriculating (although at large public universities, certain highly competitive majors such as computer science may remain capped because of space). At many private universities, the terminology of "major" and expectation of selecting one may be nonexistent altogether. Instead, they might ask about one or more "areas of interest," a completely non-binding commitment. We thus encourage applicants to be strategic in how they approach their intended fields. Going for the more selective options will make the admissions process tougher. Meanwhile, going for the less selective ones—and writing about them in your essays—just might catch the reader's attention. See "anti-stereotyping."

- **IVY LEAGUE**

  The Ivy League is a collective of eight elite, highly selective private research universities in the northeastern United States that comprises a collegiate athletic conference: Harvard University, Yale University, Princeton University, Columbia University, University of Pennsylvania, Cornell University, Brown University, and Dartmouth College. Contrary to popular belief, the Ivy League—often known informally as the "Ivies"—is not primarily an academic grouping. Its origins lie in the early days of American football, in fact. Nonetheless, the Ivies share a general identity of high-minded liberal arts thinking and intellectual rigor, along with a certain preppiness of disposition. Successful essays should speak to this culture. (Note also the many similar elite schools NOT included in this list.) See "Ivy Plus (Ivy+)."

- **IVY PLUS (IVY+)**

  "Ivy Plus" or "Ivy+" is a loose term commonly used in elite university circles to account for schools officially in the Ivy

League and those reasonably adjacent. Most would agree that by virtue of their prestige, Stanford, MIT, Caltech, UChicago, Duke, and Johns Hopkins can all be considered "Ivy Plus" schools.

- **LEADERSHIP/SERVICE PROFILE**

  Among the several basic admissions profile types that exist, the Leadership/Service Profile is defined by an emphasis on assuming organizational leadership positions (e.g. Head Boy/Girl, President of X Club) and/or enacting service-oriented projects (e.g. volunteering, social entrepreneurship).

- **LETTER OF RECOMMENDATION (LOR)**

  The Letter of Recommendation, or LOR, is a standard undergraduate application component. Universities seek to hear from an authority figure who knows you, as to gain holistic perspective on your Character/Personal Qualities. These third-party opinions can be quite helpful in weeding out the wrong kinds of candidates. After all, in submitting their LOR, your recommender is placing their stamp of approval on the words therein.

- **LIBERAL ARTS (MINDSET)**

  An often-misunderstood term, the "liberal arts" broadly means the study of all three primary academic domains—natural sciences, social sciences, and the humanities—typically with an interdisciplinary emphasis. Contrary to popular belief, the "liberal arts" does not just mean social science, humanities, or the arts. The liberal arts philosophy is what defines the majority of Western education, even when the school or environment appears rather rigid or vocational. What is the "liberal arts?" Well, it's not just the "arts" per se. Let Princeton explain for us: A liberal arts education offers an expansive intellectual grounding in all kinds of humanistic inquiry. By exploring issues, ideas and methods across the humanities and the arts, and the natural and social sciences, you will learn to read critically, write cogently and think broadly.

  —What Does Liberal Arts Mean? - Princeton University Admissions Department

  Non-American applicants may struggle with this concept, since it tends to conflict with a more straightforward STEM-oriented system such as India's. Remember that it was the ancient Greeks that formalized the idea of the seven liberal arts, teaching the quadrivium (arithmetic (number in the abstract), geometry (number in space), music (number in time), and astronomy (number in space and time)) and the trivium (grammar, logic, and rhetoric). Demonstrating appreciation for this rich tradition will demonstrate that you make a great Fit with the American academic culture.

- **LOGLINE**

  A logline is a concept used in creative industries such as film and publishing that deal in storytelling. It's a pithy sentence or two that boils down the script/manuscript to its essential elements in the form of a concise summary. When you can express your essay as a compelling logline, you have clarity about the narrative you seek to tell.

- **MAL (MOTIVATION-ACTION-LEARNING)**

  Athena's framework for approaching overall essay Structure as well as individual paragraph structure. Your reasons for doing something are your Motivation, the actions you take are your Action, and your reflections are your Learning. MAL can certainly lead to formulaic writing if you're not careful, but it's helpful in crystallizing the core of what you wish to convey. You can even look to films and see that they tend to have a three-act structure closely mirroring MAL.

- **MECE (MUTUALLY EXCLUSIVE, COLLECTIVELY EXHAUSTIVE)**

  MECE is a McKinsey coinage used to ensure that the main points of any proposed solution offered to a consulting client address all the important concerns without redundancy. Applied to college applications, MECE is critical for making the most of each application component. Your Personal Essay is in conversation with your Personal Information section, your Activity List, your LORs, and of course, your Supplements. Effective applications take advantage of how to showcase one's Hooks with a rich, reinforced theme.

- **MECHANICS**

  Within our Content, Structure, Style, and Mechanics framework, Mechanics is the final priority, defined by an essay's grammar, spelling, punctuation, and formatting—in other words, its *polish*. A successful Personal Essay must abide by English's standard conventions, for American courses are taught almost exclusively in English. You must demonstrate command over the language to be qualified—especially as an international applicant from a country where English isn't the primary or official language. In those cases, the scrutiny is higher (especially since Asian applicants often score high on logical, quantitative metrics such as the Math section of the SAT but relatively low on qualitative metrics such as Reading.)

- **PERSONAL ESSAY**

  The Personal Essay is a genre of Application Essays—specifically, the long-form essay of around 650–700 words that serves as the main essay an application will ask. Most application platforms require it, for example the CAE for the Common App, the Coalition Application Essay for the Coalition Application, the long essay for UT Austin, and so forth. What links each of these similar essays is the open-ended, free-form nature of the prompt(s). Because their focus is broadly on your Character/ Personal Qualities, they don't explicitly ask for you to provide college-specific or Intended Major-specific information. In fact, doing so might hurt your chances, since the essay is supposed to be general. For strategic purposes, you should think of the Personal Essay as an expression of your core brand—your central value-add to an incoming freshmen class—and the Supplements as additional context for that brand. If it wasn't entirely clear, the Personal Essay is the focus of this book.

  Note that *personal essay* also refers to a literary genre of creative nonfiction in which the author writes from their own voice about their lived experiences. The Application Essay version is merely an adaptation of that genre.

- **PERSONAL INFORMATION SECTION**

  Almost all college application platforms will feature a "Personal Information" section that asks for personal details such as name, birth date, gender identity, and other demographic details. This section is universities' primary means of gleaning your core uncontrollable Baskets: Citizenship, Geographic Location, Gender, Race/Ethnicity, Income Level, Alumni Relation. Your Personal Essay should be addressing these inputs, either by deepening or emphasizing them—or by engaging in antistereotyping.

- **PERSONAL STATEMENT**

   "Personal statement" is an extremely broad, thus confusing term in the Application Essay genre. Many domains use it interchangeably with Personal Essay (the CAE used to be listed as a "Personal Statement" in the Common App as recently as around 2020), but the UCAS (main application platform for UK schools) uses it for a long-form essay that's really an SOP. We thus avoid the term for the purposes of this book.

- **PERSPECTIVE**

   Within our VPAC framework, Perspective is the second priority, defined by insight, observation, and awareness. A successful Personal Essay must be appropriately reflective, else it may demonstrate Values but have nothing to say *about* those Values.

- **PIVOT**

   The Pivot is our term for that moment in the Personal Essay when the narrative clearly shifts toward the conclusion. Often, there's a big epiphany or realization, prompted by a dramatic event such as an insightful conversation with a parent or grandparent. Beware: the Pivot is a trope that can easily become predictable and formulaic. Think of it as a genre convention that can be toyed with.

- **PROFILE**

   Your admissions **Profile** is the collection of information that defines your candidacy for admission. It's a mix of "Hard Factors" (quantifiable metrics like academic grades and test scores) and "Soft Factors" (demographic or qualitative metrics like Character/Personal qualities). At its center is your human brand, the central value-add you bring to an incoming freshman class. Think of it as your resume or CV, albeit with more of a holistic emphasis.

- **PROJECT/ACTIVITY ESSAY**

   Within the set of the most common Personal Essay genres, the Project/Activity Essay is defined by its subject matter being the author's, you guessed it, project or activity. Typically, it'll be their most notable one. Aditya Mehta's CAE, featured in the sample essays chapter, is a prime example. When done right, the Project/Activity Essay can demonstrate compelling Values and Perspective in a tangible, concrete manner that avoids the broadness of a simply "personal" essay. Common dangers include formulaic approach, impersonality, and cliché.

- **RED FLAG**

    For admissions departments, a Red Flag is a concern that gives them reason to be wary of granting admission for an application. It may not necessarily lead to a denial, but admission does become less likely. Examples include: criminal activity, extremist views, falsified information, glaring typos.

- **STANDARD STRONG**

    Apparently a common term in admissions, "Standard Strong" defines an applicant who's perhaps qualified, with plenty of competitive Hard Factors and decent Soft ones, but somehow fails to stand out among their demographic. Your goal is always to distinguish yourself from the other Standard Strong applicants from your Baskets by engaging in antistereotyping with your Application Essay Writing.

- **STATEMENT OF PURPOSE (SOP)**

    The statement of purpose, or SOP, is an Application Essay genre defined by its subject matter: your intended major, course, or program. In contrast with the Personal Essay, it has a narrow focus, reflective of a more directed, specialized educational philosophy. Broadly, it falls under a wider umbrella of "Academic Essays." While the UK has been asking for a 4,000-character undergraduate SOP for years, it should come as no surprise that SOPs are typically asked in the US for specialized majors (such as art and design) or for graduate programs. In these cases, applicants are expected to be more mature and confident about their plans. This point is encompassed by the very name, statement of *purpose* instead of mere "personal statement." Note that "personal statement" often refers to some form of SOP, however.

- **STRUCTURE**

    Within our Content, Structure, Style, and Mechanics framework, Structure is the second priority, defined by an essay's organization of ideas—in other words, its *form*. A successful Personal Essay must be upheld by sturdy scaffolding that makes intuitive sense. Otherwise, it'll appear confusing and/or muddled for the reader.

- **STYLE**

  Within our Content, Structure, Style, and Mechanics framework, Style is the third priority, defined by an essay's distinct personal approach—in other words, its *literary voice*. A successful Personal Essay must be distinct in its format and language choices. Otherwise, it'll appear generic and formulaic.

- **SUPPLEMENT**

  A Supplement is an additional set of essays that an application platform may ask for beyond the standard Personal Essay. Supplements vary in length and topic, depending on the college, but one thing they share is that they're asked directly by the college. Supplements are an opportunity for admissions departments to gain more specific knowledge about your Fit with their community—academically and otherwise—which makes them an opportunity for you to showcase that Fit. Your aim should be to use the Personal Essay in such a way that doesn't later prove redundant in the Supplements. That's why the Planning stage is so crucial for your essay process.

- **THIRD-CULTURE KID**

  A third-culture kid, or "third-culture individual (TCI)," is someone who was raised in a culture different from their parents' or their citizenship/nationality. It's a pretty common basket for international applicants, who're quite accustomed to travel, relocation, and living in diverse environments. Such applicants are typically affluent, with parents who work at MNCs or diplomatic organizations; they tend to be educated at international schools with other expats.

- **TRAUMATIC EXPERIENCE ESSAY**

  Within the set of the most common Personal Essay genres, the Traumatic Experience Essay is defined by its subject matter being the author's painful lived experience, such as bullying, sexual harassment, disease, divorce/separation, and so on. Sarika Yadav's CAE, featured in the sample essays chapter, is a prime example. When done right, the Traumatic Experience Essay can demonstrate compelling Values of courage and tenacity while making for a memorable impact. Common dangers include devolution into a maudlin, navelgazing sob story. Readers may see you as a manipulator trying to pull at their heart strings.

- **UNUSUAL TRAIT/EXPERIENCE ESSAY**

  Within the set of the most common Personal Essay genres, the Unusual Trait/Experience Essay is defined by its subject matter being the author's quirky nature, habits, or anecdotes. Seerat Singh's CAE, featured in the sample essays chapter, is a prime example. When done right, the Unusual Trait/Experience Essay can offer some compelling Perspective while making for a memorable impact. Common dangers include superficiality and the appearance of falling into gimmicks.

- **VALUES**

  Within our VPAC framework, Values is the first priority, defined by beliefs, ethics, and principles. American admissions cherishes Values of Intellectual Vitality, Community/Diversity Orientation, Leadership/Ambition, Courage, and Tenacity. A successful Personal Essay must showcase at least one of these core Values, else it will feel hollow and pointless.